Andrew Edney

WINDOWS VISTA MEDIA CENTER

In easy steps is an imprint of Computer Step
Southfield Road · Southam
Warwickshire CV47 0FB · United Kingdom
www.ineasysteps.com

Notice of Liability
Every effort has been made to ensure that this book contains accurate
and current information. However, Computer Step and the author
shall not be liable for any loss or damage suffered by readers as a
result of any information contained herein.

Trademarks
Microsoft® and Windows® are registered trademarks of Microsoft
Corporation. All other trademarks are acknowledged as belonging to
their respective companies.

Printed and bound in the United Kingdom

ISBN-13 978-1-84078-331-5
ISBN-10 1-84078-331-1

Contents

12 TV & Guide Settings   173

Index

1 Windows Media Center

This chapter will introduce
Windows Media Center
and explain what versions
of Windows Vista contain
Windows Media Center and
how you can buy, upgrade or
build a PC to use it.

Windows Media Center

Windows Media Center PCs are all-in-one entertainment devices that can sit in your living room and provide all the benefits of a computer along with all the functionality of other devices, such as stereos, DVD players and personal video recorders.

It has what is commonly referred to as "the ten foot interface", which basically means that you can use it and get all the benefits from it when you are sitting ten feet away on your couch, because it has been specially designed to provide a different user experience to that of a normal computer.

A Windows Media Center PC allows you to:

- Watch and record your favorite TV shows and movies
- Listen to music, CDs and even the Radio
- Watch DVDs
- View slideshows of your photos and pictures
- Get access to exclusive online content
- Stream music and video to other rooms in your home using Windows Media Extenders, such as an Xbox 360
- Synchronize your favorite contents to a portable Media Center device
- Search a 14 day TV guide and much more

Windows Media Center is the latest version in a long line of Media Center software from Microsoft, and unlike previous versions that you could only buy preinstalled with a Media Center PC, is included as part of certain versions of Windows Vista.

There are a number of improvements over previous versions, including:

- An improved user interface with easier navigation
- Optimized for widescreen and High Definition (HD) displays
- Mouse and keyboard improvements and Tablet PC support
- An Express Setup option to enable quicker first time use

Don't forget

You don't have to use all the functionality of Windows Media Center, if you don't want to. For example, if you don't want or need to watch TV then you won't need a TV tuner card, which should reduce the amount of money you need to spend on equipment.

Hot tip

Windows Media Center now comes with a built-in MPEG-2 decoder, so you no longer have to buy a separate one.

Windows Vista Editions

There are six different editions of Microsoft Windows Vista:

- Vista Starter
- Vista Home Basic
- Vista Home Premium
- Vista Business
- Vista Enterprise
- Vista Ultimate

There are also 32-bit and 64-bit editions of Windows Vista.

Windows Media Center is only available as part of Windows Vista Home Premium and Windows Vista Ultimate editions.

Windows Vista Home Premium

Windows Vista Home Premium edition contains everything you will need to get an enhanced user experience, including:

- Built-in security including Windows Defender and Windows Firewall so you can be protected very quickly and easily
- Windows Media Center
- The new Windows Aero user interface
- Built-in DVD and CD authoring facilities
- Enhanced Windows Mobility and Tablet PC support

Windows Vista Ultimate

Windows Vista Ultimate edition is the top of the range product from Microsoft and it combines all the best features of all the other available Vista editions plus much more, including:

- Advanced backup features
- Advanced connectivity features
- BitLocker Drive Encryption for added data security
- Windows Ultimate Extras which are additional services, software and more, only available to users of Windows Vista Ultimate edition

Beware

Windows Vista Starter edition will not be available in US, Canada, the European Union, Australia, New Zealand or other high income markets.

Hot tip

You can easily upgrade Vista Home Premium to Vista Ultimate using the Windows Anytime Upgrade feature found in Control Panel.

9

Don't forget

If you want to use Windows Media Center as part of Windows Vista, you must have either Vista Home Premium or Vista Ultimate edition installed.

Getting a Media Center PC

There are a number of different options for getting a Media Center PC, including buying one that is specially designed as a Windows Media Center PC, buying a Windows Vista ready PC, upgrading an existing PC or even building one yourself.

Buying a Windows Media Center PC

This option is by far the easiest if you want a PC that has been specially designed as a Windows Media Center PC and will fit perfectly in your living room without looking like it is a PC.

Windows Media Center PCs come with Windows Vista preinstalled and have all the required hardware already available and configured, which may include a remote control, multiple TV tuner cards, sound cards, wireless keyboards and mice, and more.

There are a number of large vendors that sell Windows Media Center computers, including Dell, HP and Sony.

Buying a Windows Vista Ready PC

You can also buy a Windows Vista Ready PC which will be capable of running not only Windows Vista but also Windows Media Center. It is extremely important to note, though, that it is unlikely that a Windows Vista Ready PC will have all of the components you will need to get the most out of Windows Media Center (such as TV tuner cards and a remote control).

Any PC that displays the Windows Vista Premium Ready PC logo can run Windows Vista Home Premium, Windows Vista Business or Windows Vista Ultimate edition, as well as being able to run any of the other editions.

Windows Vista Premium Ready PCs come with at least:

- 1 GHz 32-bit (x86) or 64-bit (x64) processor

- 1 GB of system memory

- A graphics card that is Windows Aero capable (which means that it supports the Windows Display Driver Model (WDDM), has a DirectX 9-class graphics processor unit (GPU) that supports Pixel Shader 2.0 and supports 32 bits per pixel

- 128 MB of graphics memory

- 40 GB of hard drive capacity with 15 GB free space

- DVD-ROM drive

- Audio output capability

- Internet access capability

Upgrade Requirements

The following is a list of the operating systems that can be upgraded to Windows Vista Home Premium or Ultimate:

Vista Home Premium Upgrade Requirements

- Windows XP Home Edition with SP2

- Windows Vista Home Basic

- Windows XP Media Center Edition with SP2

Vista Ultimate Upgrade Requirements

- Windows XP Home Edition with SP2

- Windows XP Professional Edition with SP2

- Windows XP Media Center Edition with SP2

- Windows XP Tablet Edition with SP2

- Windows Vista Home Basic

- Windows Vista Home Premium

- Windows Vista Business

Beware

While this is the minimum specification of a Windows Vista Premium Ready PC, it is certainly not that high of a specification these days, and as such, make sure you look at something with a much better specification before you spend your money.

11

Don't forget

If you are planning on upgrading your existing operating system to Windows Vista, make sure your computer is powerful enough.

Hot tip

You might want to consider just replacing some of the components in your existing PC in order to make it compatible with Vista.

Hot tip

For the best performance consider buying multi-core or dual-core processors.

Hot tip

If you have 120 GB of storage space for media content, this is equivalent to approximately 44 hours of recordings at best quality.

Building a Media Center PC

Because you can now buy the software to run Windows Media Center, instead of having to buy a complete Media Center PC, you can easily build your own Media Center PC. You will need to buy a number of specific components along with a good quality motherboard and processor capable of running Windows Vista.

Motherboard and Processor

The minimum specification processor you need is a 1 GHz 32-bit or 64-bit processor – the higher the specification of the processor the better Windows Vista will run. Ensure the motherboard can support the processor you choose and that it has plenty of expansion slots for the different components you will need in order to get the most out of Windows Media Center.

Memory

The minimum amount of system memory is 1 GB but 2 GB (or more) would be better for Windows Media Center as some of the applications you may decide to run could be memory intensive.

Hard Drive

The minimum capacity for a supported hard drive is 40 GB. Hard drives are very cheap and the bigger the hard drive the more recordings, music and pictures you can store on your Windows Media Center. Consider buying SATA drives if your motherboard supports SATA, as they are faster. You should also consider having a separate drive only for use as Media Center storage.

DVD Drive

The minimum requirement for Windows Vista is a DVD-ROM drive, however, if you want to create CDs and DVDs of your favorite media content, then you will need a DVD Writer. Most DVD Writers on the market support both DVD + and - formats. Blu-ray drives are now beginning to make an appearance for even higher quality High Definition content.

Graphics Card

A minimum supported graphics card needs to have a graphics processor that runs Windows Aero and has 128 MB of memory. Because of the requirements of Windows Aero, a lot of older graphics cards may not be up to the task. Look for graphics cards that say they support Windows Vista. Both ATI and nVidia produce supported graphics cards. For the best picture quality look for a graphics card with either DVI connectors or preferably HDMI connectors.

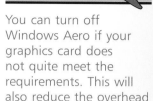

Hot tip

You can turn off Windows Aero if your graphics card does not quite meet the requirements. This will also reduce the overhead on the processor.

Sound Card

The only sound requirement for Vista is the ability to output audio, so any sound card will suffice. Depending on your environment you might require a sound card that supports Dolby Digital (both 5.1 and 7.1) and DTS. The type of connectors it has is also important so choose carefully.

13

Hot tip

Most TV Tuner cards will also come with a built-in FM Tuner for listening to the radio.

TV Tuner Cards

A TV Tuner card is required if you want to watch live TV or movies that are broadcast over the air or via Satellite or Cable. Windows Media Center can support multiple tuners so that you can watch something while recording something else. Some tuner cards even have two tuners built into a single card.

Remote Control

A Windows Media Center remote control enables you to control all the functions of Windows Media Center from the comfort of your couch.

Hot tip

Having a remote control certainly makes the whole Windows Media Center experience better, but you can also use the mouse or keyboard to control everything.

Upgrading an Existing PC

If you want to upgrade an existing PC, and it is on the supported upgrade list, then there are some simple steps to follow to ensure your PC is capable of running Windows Vista.

Windows Vista Upgrade Advisor

Windows Vista Upgrade Advisor is a free download that will check your PC by running a number of tests and answer the following questions:

- Can my PC be upgraded to Windows Vista?
- How can I fix any issues that there might be?
- What will the Vista experience be like?
- What can I do to improve that experience?

The actual assessment includes the following tests:

- System capabilities (memory, hard drive space and more)
- Device compatibility
- Application compatibility

Don't forget

You will need access to the Internet to download the Windows Vista Upgrade Advisor.

14

1 Go to http://www.microsoft.com/windowsvista/getready/ upgradeadvisor/default.mspx or

2 Place the Windows Vista installation DVD in the PC and select "Check compatibility online"

Check compatibility online

Don't forget

Make sure you have plugged in all the devices you use to ensure they are scanned by the Vista Upgrade Advisor program.

3 Click the Download Windows Vista Upgrade Advisor link and then choose a location to save it

4 When it has downloaded, double-click the file and follow the steps to install and then start up the program

5 Click on Start Scan to begin the process of analyzing both the software and hardware

6 When the scan has completed, click the See Details button to review the findings

7 Select one of the See Details boxes

8 Scroll through the list of results and review the findings for each of the tabs (System, Devices and Programs)

9 Finally select Task List and review what you need to do prior to upgrading

Performing the Upgrade

Once you have worked through the results of the Windows Vista Upgrade Advisor, the next step is to perform the upgrade itself.

1 Place the Windows Vista installation DVD in the PC while Windows is running and click on Install Now

2 Click Next and then click Go online to get the latest updates (recommended) which will enable the setup process to download and use the latest updates

3 Enter the Product Key for the version of Windows Vista you have purchased and then click Next

4 Click I accept the License Terms (required to use Windows) and then click Next

5 Click Upgrade (recommended) to perform the actual upgrade

Beware

There may be some devices or programs that are not compatible with Windows Vista – make sure you read through all the results carefully and follow any instructions or advice presented to you.

Don't forget

Make a backup of all of your important data before starting the upgrade process, just in case of any problems.

Hot tip

If you are upgrading a previous Media Center installation, scheduled recordings, recording history, installed applications and your audio and video preferences are all migrated for you.

Hot tip

If you have an Xbox 360 you can also use the Xbox 360 Media Remote Control to perform most of the functions of a standard Windows Media remote control.

Beware

While you can control Windows Media Center without a remote control, if you want to watch or record TV from a set-top box you will need an infrared receiver and blaster, in order to allow Windows Media Center to change the channels on the set-top box for you.

The Remote Control

You can control Windows Media Center with a remote control which enables you to do everything from your couch.

There are different models available of the Windows Media Center remote control with a variety of different options. If you buy a Windows Media Center PC you will get a remote control as part of the package, otherwise you can buy one.

As well as the remote control itself you will also need either an infrared receiver (IR), which is usually connected to your Windows Media Center computer via USB, or a receiver that is built into the computer and may operate on a radio frequency or even via Bluetooth.

The prominent button on a Windows Media Center remote control is known as The Green Button. This button will actually launch Windows Media Center with a single touch.

The remote may also have specific buttons that can perform the following type of functions:

- Navigation buttons for all types of playback including TV, movie and music

- One touch recording

- Shortcuts for Pictures, TV, Music

- Volume controls and mute

- DVD menu

- A More button for additional menu options

- A button to launch the Guide

- Sleep which will put the Windows Media Center PC into hibernation

- Teletext quick buttons

- A number keypad that can also be used to enter text

Other Controls

If you don't have a remote control or you also want to control Windows Media Center in other ways, you can use either the keyboard, a mouse or the onscreen controls.

Using a Mouse

You can launch Windows Media Center by using the mouse to select it from the Start Menu. You can then use the mouse to select menu items by clicking on them. If your mouse has a scroll wheel you can use it to scroll up and down through the menu. When you move the mouse the onscreen controls will appear if they are available. You can then click any of these controls to active them (such as channel - or +, play, pause or the volume controls).

Using a Keyboard

You can use a keyboard to control all of the features and functions of Windows Media Center either by using the arrow keys and ENTER or by using a variety of different keyboard shortcuts. Some of the more frequently used commands are:

Required Action	Keyboard shortcut
Launch Windows Media Center or return to the Start screen	Windows key + ALT + ENTER
Accept selection	ENTER
Go back to the previous screen	BACKSPACE
Go to Music	CTRL + M
Record a TV Show	CTRL + R
Launch the Guide	CTRL + G

The User Interface

Access to the various features of Windows Media Center is controlled through the main menu system, which is controlled by either the remote control or via a mouse and keyboard.

There are a series of headings (such as TV + Movies, Music, etc) and each one of those headings has a group of icons which control different elements within Windows Media Center.

To launch any of those elements is just a case of scrolling to the one you require and then selecting it.

The user interface has been redesigned since the previous version and now provides a much easier way of navigating the menus and finding the content you want.

Hot tip

The most enjoyable way to use Windows Media Center is with a remote control.

Beware

If you are used to using Windows Media Center 2005, some of the applications are no longer included within Windows Media Center.

Media Center 2005   Windows Media Center

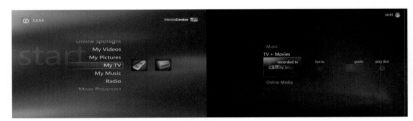

You can also control the shutdown functions for both Windows Media Center and Windows Vista itself from within the menu.

1   From the Tasks menu select Shutdown

2   You can choose from the following:

Close   Shut Down   Sleep

Log Off   Restart

2 Basic Setup

This chapter will start the setup process for Windows Media Center and perform the required setup.

Starting Setup

Windows Media Center is installed as part of the Vista operating system, so the initial step to setting up Windows Media Center is to launch it for the first time. This will begin the setup process and can actually be started in a couple of different ways. Either:

1 Either click the Start button and select Windows Media Center from the Start list

Hot tip

You may have to click on Show all items to display the Windows Media Center icon on the Welcome Center screen.

2 Or from the Welcome Center screen, click on Windows Media Center from the Get Started with Windows section and then click on Set up Windows Media Center

Express Setup

The first screen you will see is the initial welcome screen. From here you can decide whether to run the Express setup, the Custom setup or even to Run setup later.

Express setup is the simplest and quickest way to get up and running with Windows Media Center. By selecting it Windows Media Center will automatically connect to the Internet to download any artwork and information on your media and will also sign you up to the Customer Experience Improvement Program.

Hot tip

Unless you are really in a rush, always choose the Custom setup as it gives you more options to choose from.

1 Select which setup option you want to use by either using the remote control (if you have one connected), the keyboard or a mouse, ensuring the radio button is selected

2 Click on the OK button

Windows Media Center will now be configured and will be ready to use.

You can now start to explore all of the various features of Windows Media Center by scrolling through the menu choices and selecting something that interests you.

You can also configure some of the other options, such as the speakers and the TV signal, if you have one to connect.

Hot tip

You can run setup again at anytime from Tasks, Settings, General, Windows Media Center Setup and selecting Run Setup Again. This will take you directly to Custom setup. If you want to see the initial setup again, just close Windows Media Center after selecting Run Setup Again and restart it.

Custom Setup

Custom Setup enables you to choose a number of the Windows Media Center options. It takes a little longer than Express Setup but it is worth doing to ensure your Windows Media Center is setup exactly the way you want it to be.

It contains two sections, Required Setup and Optional Setup. The rest of this chapter is devoted to Required Setup.

Don't forget

In order to read the online privacy statements, your computer needs to be connected to the Internet.

1 From the Welcome to Windows Media Center screen, click the Next button to begin

2 You will see the setup section information screen – just click Next

3 This screen is the Windows Media Center Privacy Statement. If you want to read the statement click on the View the Privacy Statement Online button, otherwise click Next

4 You will then be asked if you wish to join the Customer Experience Improvement Program. If you decide to join, anonymous reports will be sent, from time to time, to Microsoft from your Windows Media Center. Choose whether to join or not and then click Next

You can also read the privacy statement from here if you wish.

Enhanced Playback

By selecting Enhanced Playback you can enable Windows Media Center to connect to the Internet in order to automatically download various content for you, including:

- Cover artwork for CDs and DVDs

- TV listings information for The Guide

- Music and Movie information

1 Select whether or not you want to use this feature and click Next to continue

Enhanced Playback   Windows Media Center

Get the Most from Windows Media Center

Windows Media Center can connect to the Internet to get cover art for albums and DVDs, music and movie information, TV Program Guide listings to schedule recordings, and Internet Services. Read our privacy statement to learn more.

Online Windows Media Center Privacy Statement

Do you want to periodically connect to the Internet to download this content to improve your Windows Media Center experience?

● Yes
○ No

Back   Next   Cancel

2 Click Next to complete the Required Components Setup, it will take you to the Optional Setup menu

The various parts of the Optional Setup are covered in the next chapter.

If you don't want to perform any of those steps just yet, select the I am Finished radio button and click Next and then Finish to take you to the Windows Media Center main menu and from there you can either explore Windows Media Center or you can choose to configure other options.

Wireless Networking

If you are using a wireless network connection for your Vista computer, during the initial setup you may be asked if you want to join a wireless network. If you have not done so at this point, it is a good idea to use this wizard to easily join your existing wireless network.

Don't forget

If you have already connected the computer to your wireless network before you started the Media Center Setup, you will not be asked to connect again.

1 When asked if you would like to use the Join Wireless Network Wizard, select the Yes button and click Next

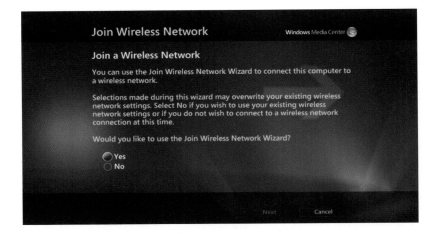

Don't forget

Your wireless network must be operational for you to connect your Vista computer to it.

2 When asked if you want to connect to your wireless network, select the Yes button and click Next

Beware

Any settings made here will overwrite any existing network settings you already have, so if you are unsure, check before continuing.

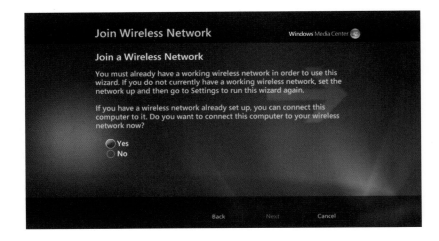

3 The next step is to select your wireless network from the list of available networks. Select the network name that corresponds to your wireless network and then click Next

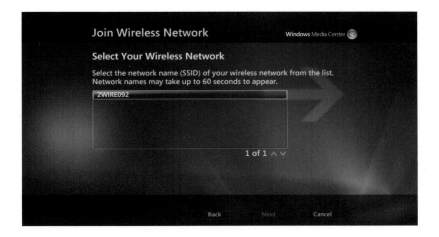

4 Type your WEP password or WPA passkey and click Next

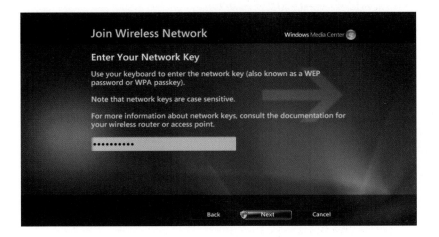

5 After successfully connecting to your network, click Next

6 Click Finish to return to the menu

Don't forget

Network keys are case sensitive, so if the key is not accepted, check if the CAPS Lock is on and try again.

25

Hot tip

You can run the Join a Wireless Network wizard at any time from Tasks, Settings, General, Windows Media Center Setup and selecting the Join Wireless Network option.

Internet Connection

During the initial setup you may be asked to set up your Internet connection. This is to help Media Center determine how the computer is connected, either "Always On" or manually.

Having an "Always On" connection is useful to download Program Guide updates and other information without you having to do anything.

1 When presented with the Set Up Your Internet Connection screen, click Next to begin configuration

2 If your computer is connected to a cable or DSL modem, or other broadband device select Yes and click Next

Beware

Make sure you are running Antivirus software and that you keep your computer up to date with security patches, especially if your computer is always connected to the Internet.

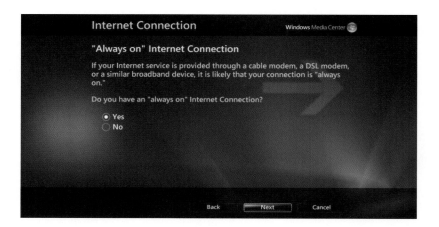

3 Click the Test button to check the connection then click Next and then click Finish to return to the menu

Hot tip

You can run the Internet Connection wizard at any time from Tasks, Settings, General, Windows Media Center Setup and then selecting the Set Up Internet Connection option.

3 Advanced Setup

This chapter will guide you through the Advanced Setup options, including how to set up TV signals from different sources, eg. through set-top boxes. It will also detail how to set up the Guide for programming information.

Optional Setup

Now that you have completed the Basic setup of Windows Media Center, the next step is the Optional Setup wizard which is considered to be some of the more advanced settings options.

Optional Setup gives you the opportunity to set up and configure the following:

- Set up and configure any TV tuners you may have installed, TV signals you can receive and the Guide

- Optimize the picture and how it is displayed on Windows Media Center

- Set up and test your speakers to ensure they work correctly

- Set up which folders Windows Media Center will watch, for any media files you want to use

1 Select the option you want to configure and click Next

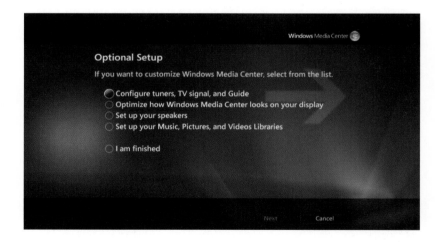

2 When you have been through all the wizards you want to setup, select I am finished and click Next

3 Click Finish to take you to the main Windows Media Center menu

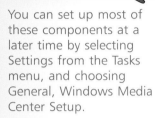

Hot tip

You can set up most of these components at a later time by selecting Settings from the Tasks menu, and choosing General, Windows Media Center Setup.

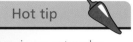

Hot tip

There is no set order in which you have to complete any of these wizards, so feel free to jump between them as you see fit.

Regions

The region setting is very important in order to ensure your Windows Media Center computer has the correct configuration information for the local television services in your country.

1 If the region that is displayed is the region you are in, select Yes, use this region to configure TV services and click Next

Hot tip

The default region should be chosen automatically as the region selected during your installation and configuration of Windows Vista.

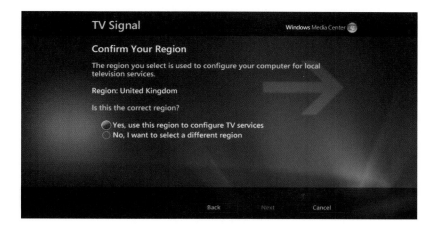

2 If not, select No, I want to select a different region and click Next

3 Select the correct region from the list and click Next

Don't forget

The type of TV signal you can receive is dependent on the type of TV tuner card you have installed in your Windows Media Center computer.

Beware

Any High Definition (HD) signal that is transmitted through either a cable or satellite set-top box is converted to standard definition.

Beware

Some premium cable channels contain protected content that cannot be recorded using Windows Media Center.

Supported TV Signals

Windows Media Center supports a number of different TV signals, including those provided by digital and analog antennas, cable TV and satellite TV sources.

Both standard and high-definition TV (HDTV) signals that are broadcast over-the-air to an antenna are supported, providing you are in an area that can receive HDTV signals.

Standard Definition TV

In order to be able to watch or record a standard definition TV signal, you will need an antenna connected to your Windows Media Center computer and a TV tuner card that supports standard definition TV. You can also connect a cable TV set-top box or satellite set-top box to provide signals.

High-Definition TV

In order to be able to watch or record a high-definition TV signal, you will need a TV tuner card that supports a digital TV signal, such as DVB-T or ATSC.

If you are in the United States, you may need a Digital Cable Tuner device and a subscription to a digital cable provider in order to watch and record over-the-air high-definition TV.

Supported Standards

Some of the supported standards include:

ATSC

Stands for Advanced Television Systems Committee who have developed a new digital standard in the United States. Canada, Mexico and Korea have also adopted this standard. Window Media Center currently only supports ATSC for the United States and Korea.

QAM

Stands for Quadrature Amplitude Modulation and is the digital cable standard in the United States. Windows Media Center supports QAM signals with a Digital Cable Tuner in the United States.

DVB-T

Digital Video Broadcasting is the European standard for digital terrestrial TV. Windows Media Center supports DVB-T in all locales.

TV Signal Setup

Once you have confirmed which region you are in, Windows Media Center will download the latest TV setup options for your computer based on your selection. These options can vary for different regions.

The next step is to select the source of the TV signal you currently receive and want to use. These sources include:

- Cable

- Satellite

- Antenna (Analog or Digital)

1 Select Configure my TV signal automatically (recommended) and click Next to continue

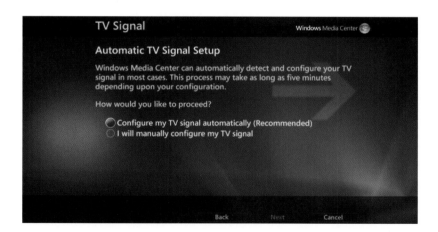

The Automatic TV Signal Setup will scan for all types of input for your TV capture cards, including Cable, Set-top Box and Antenna. This process can take up to 5 minutes, so be patient.

If the scan fails you can choose to manually configure your TV signal, otherwise skip ahead to step 6.

2 Select Manually configure the TV signal

3 Click Next to continue

Don't forget

If you don't have a TV tuner card installed in your Window Media Center computer you will not be able to access these setup wizards.

Hot tip

If Windows Media Center gives you the option to configure your TV signal automatically take it – it is much easier and quicker to do it this way.

...cont'd

If Windows Media Center cannot detect a TV signal you should check that you have a working signal before continuing.

④ Select the source of the TV signal you want to use

⑤ Click Next to continue

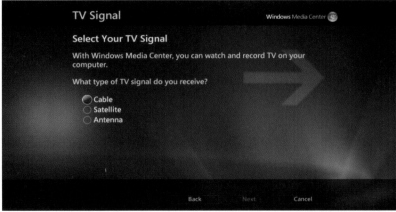

Hot tip

If you have multiple TV tuner cards installed in your Windows Media Center PC make sure you configure them all.

The next step is only applicable if you have more than one TV tuner card installed in your Windows Media Center computer.

If you only have one TV tuner card, skip ahead to step 7.

⑥ Select which of tuners you want to configure, and click Next to continue

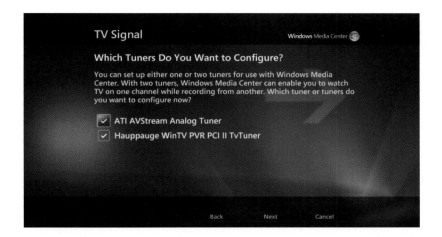

Hot tip

If you are using multiple tuners, you can use a cable splitter so that you can connect it into both tuner cards.

Don't forget

If you are using multiple tuners, each tuner card will need its own TV signal source.

(7) Before continuing, make sure of the following:

● If you are using a set-top box that it is switched on

● The IR control cable (if you have and need one) is connected and correctly positioned

● Your Windows Media Center computer is connected to your selected TV source or sources

There are a number of different connections that could be used to connect your TV source or sources to your Windows Media Center computer. These include:

● S-Video connections

● Composite Video

What is available for you to use will be dependent on what connections your TV source supports and what connections your TV tuner card supports. For example, if your set-top box has composite video connections, then the TV tuner card must be able to accept composite video connections. You might also be able to get a cable that can convert one type of connection to another.

Hot tip

S-Video is much better quality that Composite, so where possible try to connect via S-Video.

(8) Click Next to continue on to selecting TV sources

33

Selecting TV Sources

Don't forget

If you are using multiple TV tuners, you will need to repeat this process for each TV tuner. Make sure you have connected the correct TV signal source into the correct TV tuner.

When the Select a Working TV Signal screen first appears, Windows Media Center will automatically scan all the available connections to see if it can find a signal.

If it does, the connection will automatically be selected and a real-time image of whatever is being broadcast will appear in a small window to the side of the available choices. Click Next to continue.

Hot tip

If the TV signal is not automatically detected, try selecting each of the relevant connections in turn until it is detected.

Select your Set-top Box Brand

You may be asked to tell Windows Media Center the make of your set-top box. If you are asked, scroll through the list of set-top box brands and select your box then click Next.

Hot tip

Don't worry if your set-top box is not listed, try and pick something that looks similar and see if it works and if not pick something else.

Set-top Box Remote Controls

If you use a set-top box to provide a TV signal to your Windows Media Center computer, you will have the opportunity to use your set-top box remote control as well.

1 If you control your set-top box with a remote control, select Yes, and then click Next

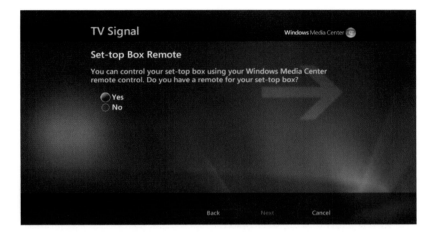

Hot tip

If you are using any type of universal remote control, ensure you have it set to set-top box mode before continuing.

2 Windows Media Center will attempt to identify your remote control by asking you to press and hold a series of buttons. Perform these button steps as prompted, you might be asked to repeat some of them

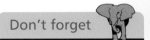

Don't forget

Make sure you have your set-top box remote control to hand and that you have a clear line of sight to the set-top box itself from wherever you are seated.

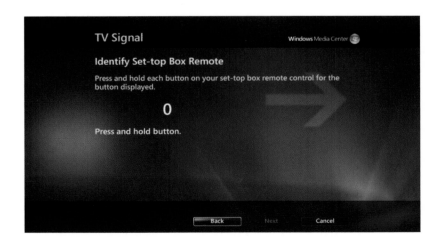

...cont'd

At this point, your set-top box remote should be recognized and you will see a screen that will tell you as much.

 3 Click Next to move on to the set-top box Configuration

Learning a Remote Control

If the set-top box remote is not recognized, Windows Media Center can learn the functions of the remote control with some help from you.

1 Select Have Windows Media Center learn my remote from scratch and click Next

2 You will be asked if your set-top box remote control has a button, such as Enter or OK which is used to change channels. Select either Yes, it does or No, it does not depending on the remote and then click Next to continue

3 The next steps involve pressing and holding a number of buttons on the remote control in turn so that Windows Media Center can learn them. Complete each one as directed – you may be asked to repeat some of them – don't worry as this is normal while Windows Media Center learns the functions of your remote control

Set-top Box Configuration

The next step is to inform Windows Media Center how you use your set-top box and then to test that Windows Media Center is able to change the channels for you, including a test to check the IR signal speed.

1 Select the number of digits that the highest channel you can receive has, then click Next

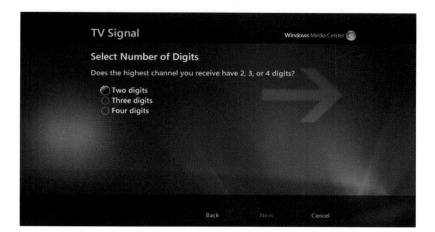

Beware

You will not be able to continue unless you have an IR blaster cable connected to your Windows Media Center computer and attached to the IR sensor on the set-top box.

2 Select whether or not you have to press either the ENTER or the OK button on your remote control after entering a channel number, then click Next to continue

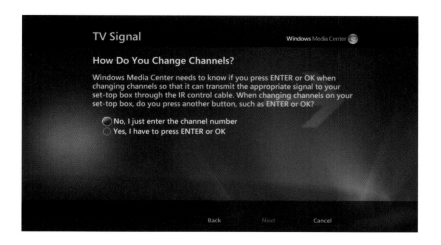

...cont'd

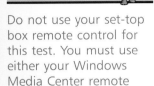

Don't forget

Do not use your set-top box remote control for this test. You must use either your Windows Media Center remote control or the keyboard.

Hot tip

If the channel did not change correctly, check that the IR blaster cable is correctly positioned over the IR sensor on your set-top box and try the test again.

Hot tip

Make sure you have a clear line of sight to the Windows Media Center computer or IR blaster box when performing this test.

3 Using either the keyboard or the Windows Media Center remote control, enter a channel number you know works

4 If the channel changed correctly (as displayed in the little window), select The set-top box changed the channel correctly and click Next to continue

5 Using the channel up and down buttons on the Windows Media Center remote control, change the channels at least six times and select if the channel changed correctly. Then click Next twice to continue

Scanning for Services

This option is only required if one or more of your TV signal sources is from an Antenna. If you are not using an Antenna for your signal source, move on to Setting Up the Guide.

1 Select Configure my TV signal automatically and click Next

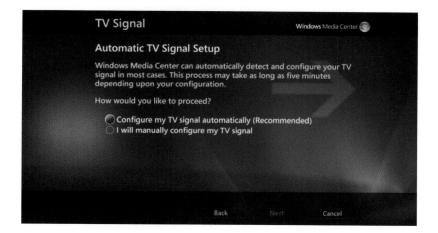

2 If you are using multiple tuners, select which tuner you want to configure

3 If the automatic setup fails, select whether you are using Analog terrestrial or Digital terrestrial, then click Next

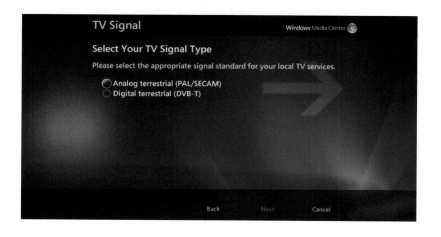

Hot tip

Windows Media Center supports both Analog terrestrial and Digital terrestrial sources.

39

Don't forget

In the United Kingdom, Analog terrestrial TV is being switched off from early 2008.

...cont'd

4 Click Next again

5 Select Start Scan to search for all available services (this can take quite a while)

At the end of the scanning process, you will see the number of services found, along with a list of the names of those TV channels.

Scroll through the list to see if there are any that are missing.

Hot tip

If there are any channels missing even after performing a rescan, don't worry, you can attempt to add these later from the Settings menu so that you have a complete line up.

6 If you believe that there are any channels missing from the services found, select the Scan for more to repeat the scanning process

7 Click Next to complete the set up and move on to Setting Up the Guide

Setting Up the Guide

The Guide provides 14 days worth of TV listings for your available channels. It helps you to find your favorite shows, watch them and even record them to watch again at a later time.

1 Click Next to start

2 Select Yes to signify that you want to use the Guide and click Next

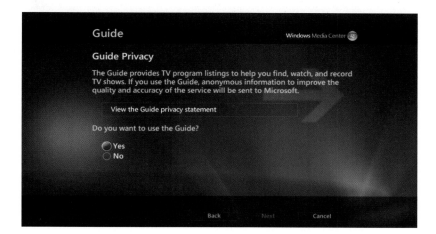

3 Select I Agree to the Guide terms of use and click Next

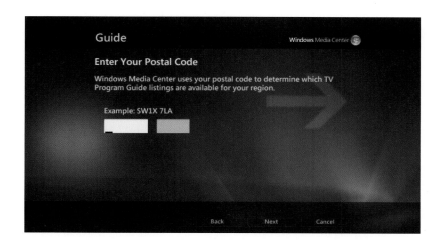

Don't forget

Depending on where you are in the world, this may appear as either Postal Code or Zip Code.

4 Enter your Postal Code or Zip Code and click Next

Your Windows Media Center computer will now connect to the Internet to download provider information. This information is specific to the local area you live in.

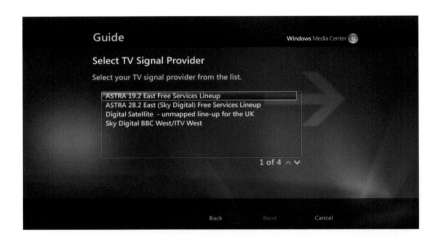

Hot tip

If your TV Signal Provider is not listed for some reason, select the one that most closely matches.

5 Select the TV Signal Provider that matches your actual provider then click Next to begin downloading Guide information (this may take a few minutes, so be patient)

6 After the download is complete, click Next

Don't forget

Your Windows Media Center computer needs to be connected to the Internet in order to download the Guide information.

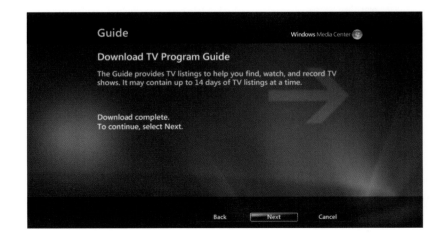

Setting Up Speakers

The next step is to set up your speakers. From here you will specify the number of speakers connected to your Windows Media Center computer and have the opportunity to test that they are working correctly.

There are three possible speaker configurations to choose from:

- 2 speakers
- 5.1 surround speakers
- 7.1 surround speakers

1 Select Set up your speakers from the Optional Setup menu

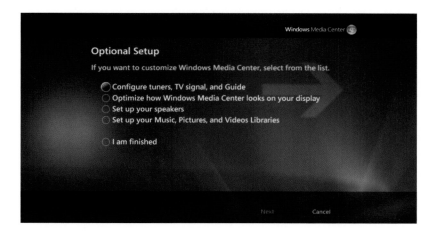

2 From the Welcome to Speaker Setup page, click Next

The next step is to select the type of connection you are using for the connection between your Windows Media Center computer and your speakers. The choices include:

- Mini-plug and Dual RCA (for analog connections)
- Single RCA and Toslink (for digital connections)

3 Select the speaker connection type and click Next

...cont'd

Hot tip

You may only see the Speaker Connection Type screen if you have already connected a speaker connection cable to your Windows Media Center computer.

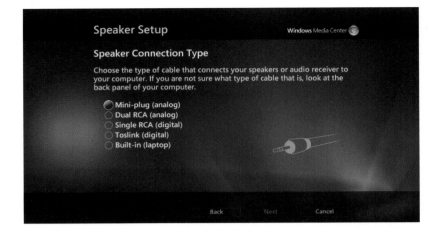

4 Choose the number of speakers that you have from the available list and click Next

Hot tip

Your exact speaker setup may not be shown, so select the number of speakers that most closely matches what you have.

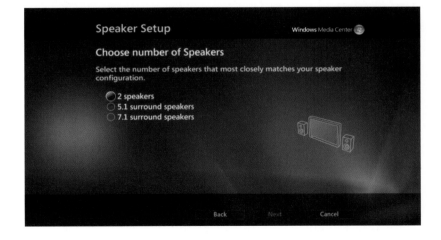

5 Click the Test button in order to test each of your connected speakers

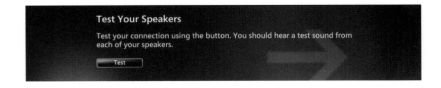

6 If you heard sound coming from each of your speakers, select the I heard sound from all of my speakers button and click Next to complete the setup. If you didn't hear sound, select the I did not hear sound from all of my speakers button and click Next for some troubleshooting steps

45

Troubleshooting Your Speakers

If you did not hear sound from all of your speakers, there are a couple of things you can check:

- Did you select the correct number of speakers?

- Are all the cables connected correctly to your speakers?

- Are the speakers connected to your computer correctly?

- Is your sound card working correctly?

- Are all the drivers installed?

- Is the sound in Windows muted?

Once you have checked all the above, you can click the Back button and rerun the speaker tests. If after checking the above list you still cannot hear sound you might have a problem with your speakers.

Media Discovery

Windows Media Center automatically watches a number of set folders for any media files. These folders are Music, Pictures and Videos.

You may want to have Windows Media Center watch other folders apart from these.

These folders can be located on your Windows Media Center computer, a shared folder on another computer on your home network or even both.

Whenever you add media files into these watched folders, they will be available from within Windows Media Center to view, watch or listen to.

To Watch a Folder on this computer

Setting up a folder to watch is both quick and easy.

1 Select Set up your Music, Pictures and Videos Libraries from the Optional Setup menu and click Next

2 Select Add folder to watch and click Next

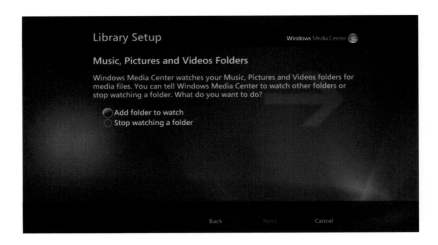

3 Select Add folders on this computer, and click Next

Hot tip

You can rerun the Library setup again at anytime from Tasks, settings, Library Setup.

Don't forget

In order to play back videos or music correctly, you will need to have the correct codecs installed on your computer.

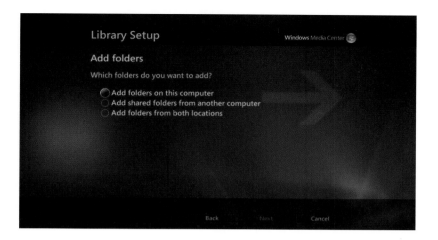

4 Select which folders you want to add by clicking on the empty box next to the name which adds a check mark, and then click Next to continue

Click the + button next to the folder name to expand the folder structure so that you only select the individual folder or folders you want to watch.

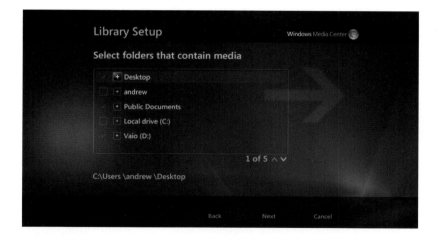

Don't forget

Folders that have a check mark against them are already shared.

5 Confirm that the folder or folders to be added are correct and if they are click Finish to add them

To Stop Watching a Folder

Hot tip

You can continue to use the Windows Media Center computer while the folders are being added if you want to.

1 Select Stop watching a folder and click Next

...cont'd

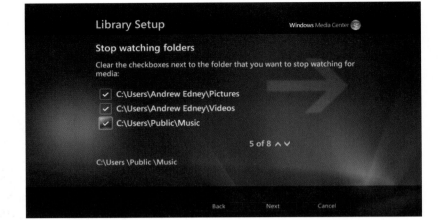

Don't forget

When you stop watching a folder, the folder and its contents are not deleted. If you want to delete the folder or any of its contents you must do it manually.

2 Clear the check boxes for the folders you want to stop watching and click Next, then confirm that the folder or folders are correct and click Finish to stop watching them

To Watch a Folder on Another Computer

1 Select Add shared folders from another computer and click Next

Don't forget

Folders you want to watch on another computer must be available during the setup process.

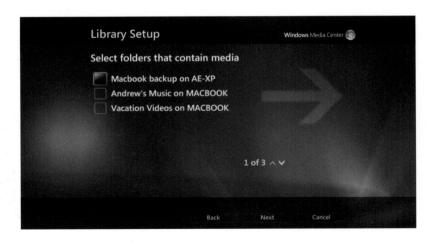

2 Select the folders that contain media and click Next, then confirm the folders are correct and click Finish

4 Displays

This chapter will guide you through the various display settings, including how to get the optimum picture from your chosen display.

Display Configuration

If you want to change the way Windows Media Center looks on your selected display, the Display Configuration wizard can help by walking you through a number of different configuration steps and showing you videos to help you determine if you have made all the necessary changes.

1 Select Optimize how Windows Media Center looks on your display and click Next

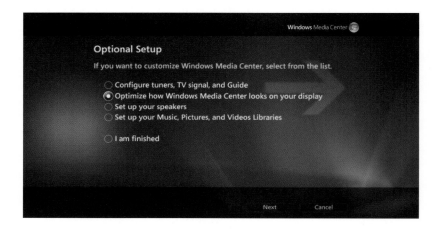

2 Select the Watch Video button to view a sample video which will show the quality of the video on your display, but will also tell you about the next few steps

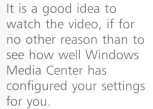

Hot tip

It is a good idea to watch the video, if for no other reason than to see how well Windows Media Center has configured your settings for you.

Beware

To get the best results, ensure you are viewing Windows Media Center in full screen mode when running through these and other configuration options.

3 Click Next to continue

Because it is very important to run through these steps when you are connected to the display that you will be using with Windows Media Center, you are asked to confirm if you are viewing this wizard on that display.

If you are not connected to your preferred display you should connect to it now and rerun this wizard before continuing.

4 Select Yes, I see the wizard on my preferred display and click Next

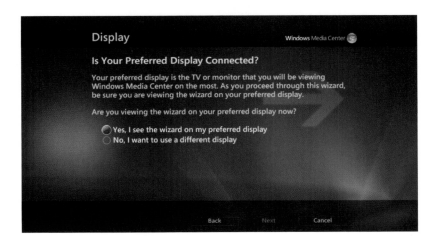

Display Types

The next step is to select the type of display that is connected to your Windows Media Center computer. When you select a particular display type, Windows Media Center makes a number of setting changes for you.

The available choices are:

Hot tip

You will notice that the image on the right-hand side of the screen changes depending on what you select, to give you a visual representation of your choices.

- Monitor (a standard computer monitor)

- Built-in Display (such as a laptop screen)

- Flat Panel (such as a Plasma or LCD screen)

- Television

- Projector

1 Select the display you have connected to Windows Media Center and click Next

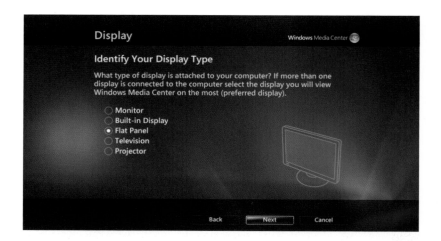

Hot tip

The highest quality connection can be made using HDMI (as long as your display and your graphics card can support it).

You then have to select the type of cable that is used to connect your chosen display to your Windows Media Center.

The available choices are:

- Composite or S-Video

- DVI, VGA or HDMI

- Component (YPbPr)

...cont'd

2   Select your Connection Type and click Next

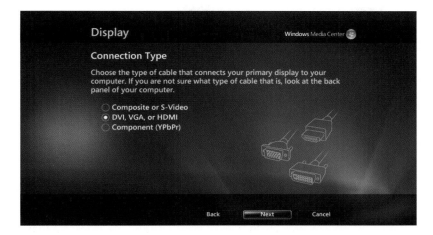

Beware

Depending on the Display Type you selected, you may not see the Connection Type screen. Don't worry, this is meant to happen!

You then have to select the Display Width of your chosen display.

The available choices are:

- Standard (4:3)
- Widescreen (16:9)

3   Select your Display Width and click Next

Hot tip

Even though your display may be Widescreen, you can sometimes get better results by selecting Standard. Try both settings to see which works best for you.

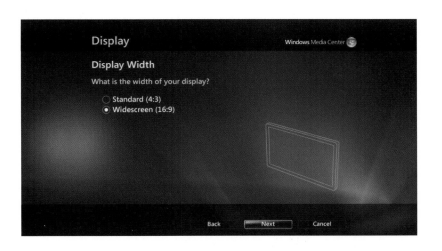

Adjusting Display Resolution

The next step is to adjust the resolution of your chosen display. This will give you the best possible combination of picture and text quality when displayed in full screen mode.

 1 Choose whether to keep the current display resolution or not, then click Next

Hot tip

Windows Media Center usually selects the best resolution for your chosen display, so you will probably keep the current display resolution, but it never hurts to check for yourself.

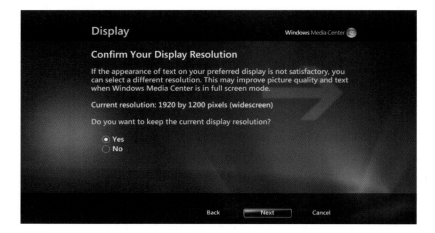

2 If you chose not to keep the current display resolution you will be presented with a list of available resolutions. Select the resolution you want to try and click Next, then choose whether to preview the adjustments.

Hot tip

Make sure you click the List All Modes option from the list to see all supported display resolutions.

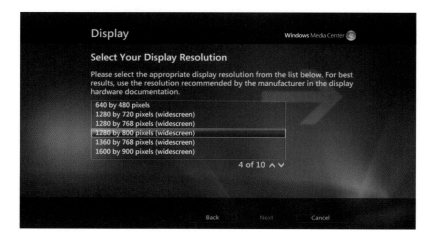

Adjusting Display Settings

You will then be presented with the opportunity to have Windows Media Center assist you in adjusting the brightness, contrast, and other settings that your display will use.

This is very useful to help you make subtle changes that otherwise might be difficult to achieve.

1 Select the Adjust display controls button and click Next

2 Click Next again to take you to the Display Calibration menu

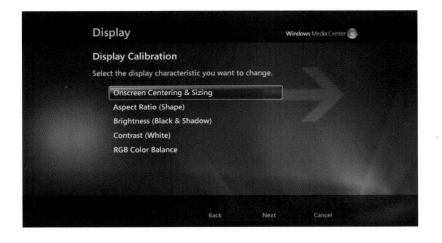

Don't forget

The display setting adjustments are all performed on your display and as such, you must be familiar with making those adjustments. If you are not, take a look at the manual that came with your display.

Hot tip

Work through each one of these options – it may be time consuming but at the end of the process you may have a better picture on your display.

Onscreen Centering & Sizing

This setting helps you to set the position of the picture on your display screen by showing you a video of a group of people playing billiards with a picture in the picture showing you the ideal setting and allowing you to adjust your setting at the same time.

Beware

You must watch the video, even if it is only for a few seconds before you will be allowed to click Next.

56

1 Select Onscreen Centering & Sizing and click Next twice, then select Watch Video to view the video

2 Using the controls on your display, adjust the sizing and centering of the video to match the inset video, then click Next to return to the Display Calibration menu

Aspect Ratio (Shape)

This setting helps you to change how shapes appear on your display screen by showing you a video of a billiards table and the white ball moving across the table.

1 Select Aspect Ratio (Shape) and click Next twice

2 Click the Watch Video button to view the video

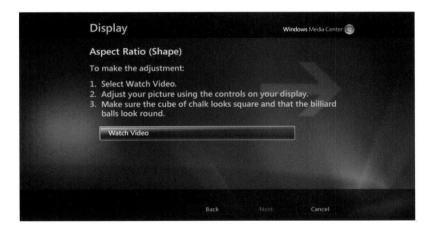

3 Using the controls on your display, make sure the cube of chalk appears square and the billiard balls look round, then click Next to return to the Display Calibration menu

Don't forget

Press the Back button on the remote control to stop the video.

Brightness (Black & Shadow)

This setting helps you to adjust the clarity of the dark colors and shadows on your display screen by showing you a video of a man chalking a billiard cue.

1 Select Brightness (Black & Shadow) and click Next twice

2 Click the Watch Video button to view the video

3 Using the brightness controls on your display, adjust the brightness of the video then click Next to return to the Display Calibration menu

Hot tip

Ensure the suit appears black and that the X behind the man has disappeared.

Contrast (White)

This setting helps you to adjust the level and clarity of the color white on your display screen by showing you a video of a man wearing a white shirt in front of a black and white wall.

1   Select Contrast (White) and click Next twice

2   Click the Watch Video button to view the video

3   Using the contrast controls on your display, set the contrast as high as possible then click Next to return to the Display Calibration menu

Hot tip

You want to set the contrast as high as possible without losing the wrinkles and buttons on the shirt.

RGB Color Balance

This setting helps you to adjust how colors appear on your display by showing you a number of different shades of gray bars on a wall.

1 Select RGB Color Balance and click Next twice

2 Click the Watch Video button to view the video

3 Using the controls on your display make any adjustments then click Next to return to the Display Calibration menu and Next again to return to the Optional Setup Menu

Hot tip

Ensure that none of the gray bars have any tinge of red, green or blue.

5 TV and Movies

This chapter will guide you through watching both Live and Recorded TV, along with being able to search for whatever you want to watch and schedule recordings where necessary. It will also explain about using Windows Media Center to watch DVDs.

Watching TV

Windows Media Center enables you to watch TV and movies from the comfort of your couch or armchair. You can watch live TV and even pause and rewind it without having previously set the show to record. You can choose to record a show or any program in a series, all with a touch of a button on the remote control.

Live TV

You can watch whatever TV show or movie is currently playing on any of the channels you can receive.

Hot tip

You can pause Live TV so that you don't miss anything if you get interrupted. You can then rewind and fast forward through the temporary recording.

1 Select Live TV from the TV + Movies menu

Hot tip

You can also watch Live TV by pressing the Live TV button at any time on the remote control.

You will then see the first channel that is available along with any information provided by the Guide (such as program title, channel and the start & end times).

2 Use the Channel + and - buttons on the remote control to change the channel

3 Press the More button on the remote control to display the options menu

These options include displaying program info, recording the program or any in the series, zoom, launching teletext or showing the mini guide.

Hot tip

You can quickly go to the last channel you were watching by pressing the Enter button on the remote control.

4 Select Mini Guide to see brief information about the show or

Don't forget

You can use your remote control to change the volume or mute it.

5 Select Program Info to see complete details about the show that is currently airing

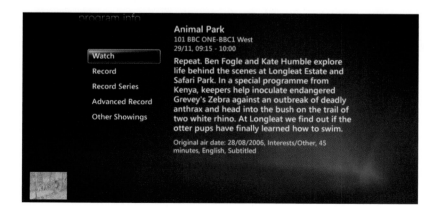

Hot tip

You can use Teletext if it is available, by either selecting Teletext from the options menu or by pressing TXT on the remote control.

6 If you want to return to the show select Watch

Recording Live TV

You can easily have Windows Media Center record the TV show you are watching or another TV show that is currently airing for you. There are a couple of different ways of recording Live TV:

Hot tip

You can easily see if a show is being recorded by the red circle that appears by the channel numbers.

1 When you are watching the program you want to record press the More button on the remote control

2 Select Record to begin recording it

3 Or just press the Record button on the remote control

Stopping a Recording

When the show you are recording has finished you can stop the recording or let it carry on if you wish.

Beware

If you only have one tuner card in your Windows Media Center computer and you change the channel while you are recording, the recording will continue with whatever channel you change to.

1 Press the More button on the remote control and select Stop Recording from the menu or

2 Press the Stop button on the remote control

Beware

Some TV shows and Movies may have copy protection and so Windows Media Center may not be able to record them for you.

3 Confirm that you want to stop the recording by selecting Yes from the dialog box

Recording a Series

A very useful feature of Windows Media Center is the ability to record a series. This means that you no longer have to manually set up a recording each time your favorite shows are on. The Series Record feature will automatically record every showing of the selected series.

1 When you are watching a show you want to record the series of, press the More button on the remote control and select Record Series

2 Press the More button again and select Series Info

You will then see all the scheduled recordings for that show, including the air date.

3 Select one of the shows that is scheduled to record

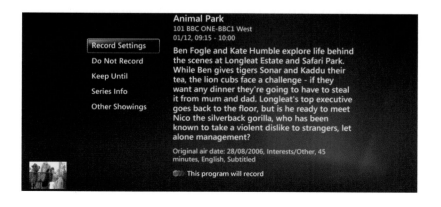

...cont'd

Should you decide, for whatever reason, you do not want to record that particular episode you can set Windows Media Center to effectively ignore it when it airs.

4 Select Do Not Record and that episode will be ignored

Series Settings

You can specify settings for a particular series that will only effect that series and no other records.

1 Select Series Settings if you are on the Series Info page or

2 Record Settings followed by Settings for the entire series if you are on the Program Info page

You can change a number of settings, including:

- Stop (either on time or for set periods afterwards)
- Quality (from Best down to Fair)
- Show Type (Live, First Run or First Run & rerun)
- Channels (the current channel only or all channels)
- Keep settings (including how many to keep and when)

3 Make your changes and click Save

Hot tip

You can also specify settings for a particular episode of a series, as well as for the whole series, by selecting Settings for this episode only from the Record Settings menu.

The Guide

Windows Media Center provides a 14 day Electronic Programming Guide that is simply referred to as the Guide. The Guide provides information for all of the channels that you have available to you, including start and end times and a description of the TV show or Movie, if one is available.

1   Select Guide from the TV + Movies menu

Hot tip

You can also access the Guide by pressing the Guide button on the remote control.

Scroll through the Guide vertically to move between channels and horizontally to move between times.

2   Highlight a timeslot to see some brief information and then select it to change the channel and watch it

Hot tip

You can also scroll through the Guide using the arrow buttons that appear on the bottom right of the screen if using a mouse or keyboard.

...cont'd

Channel Listings

If you select one of the channels you will be presented with a view of everything that is airing on that day.

1 Select a channel from the list to view available shows

Categories

You can filter the Guide by categories in order to only display the program information for selected types of show.

1 Click Categories to display the list of categories you can use to filter the Guide listings

2 Select a category to filter the Guide listings

3 Select the All category to return to the full Guide listings

Recording from the Guide

You can easily record something from the Guide by pressing the More button on the remote control and selecting either Record to record the selected show or movie, or Record Series to record the entire series of the selected show.

Recorded TV

Any TV shows or Movies that Windows Media Center has recorded for you are available to select from within the Recorded TV option in the TV + Movies Menu. From here you can watch one or more of the recorded content, set recordings, view schedules and more.

Hot tip

Recorded TV and Movies are stored as a .DVR-MS file so you can easily search for them on your Windows Media Center computer if you want to back them up.

1 Select Recorded TV from the TV + Movies menu

You will then see all of the recorded TV shows and movies sorted by the date they were recording (which is the default view).

2 Scroll through the recorded content and select something to watch

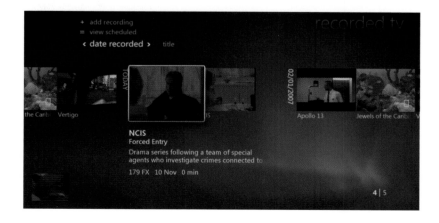

69

...cont'd

3 Review the information and then select Play to begin

If you want to see how much time has passed and how much is left on the recording, press the Pause button on the remote control to see the time span bar.

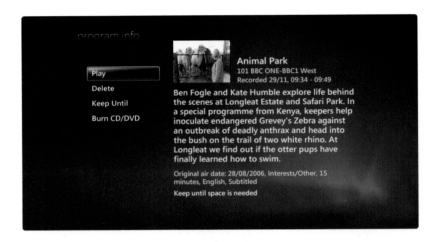

4 If you want to change the view in the Recorded TV menu press the More button on the remote control and select View List

Hot tip

The View List is useful if you have a large amount of recorded content stored on your Windows Media Center computer.

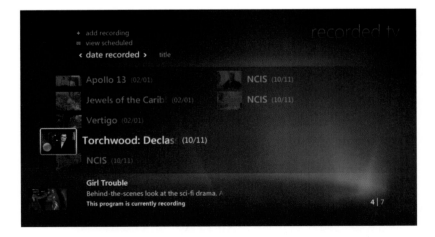

If you press the More button on the remote control you will see the additional menu items, including the ability to burn the selected show or movie to DVD, and also to view Program Info (for a TV show) or Movie Info (for a recorded movie).

Adding a Recording

An addition to recording a show when it is airing or by selecting it from the Guide, there are a number of other ways of adding a recording using Windows Media Center.

1 Select Add Recording from the Recorded TV menu

Search
The Search function enables you to search for TV shows or Movies by either Title, Keyword or Categories.

1 Select Search from the Add Recording menu

Hot tip

If you know what the TV show or Movie is called, use the Title option otherwise use the Keyword option for a quick result.

2 Select either Title, Keyword or Categories

3 Enter your search parameters and then select the result you want, then select the episode followed by Record

Custom Recording

You can also create custom recordings either by setting Windows Media Center to record a specific channel at a specified time or by keywords, including by Actor or Director.

Channel and Time

You can use the Channel and Time option to record something instead of selecting it from the Guide.

1 Select Channel and Time from the Add Recording menu

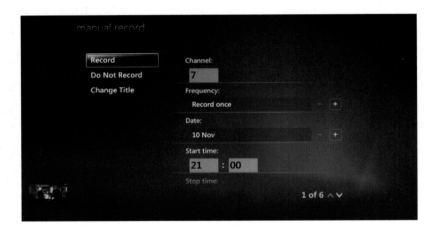

manual record

Record	Channel:
Do Not Record	7
Change Title	Frequency:
	Record once
	Date:
	10 Nov
	Start time:
	21 : 00
	Stop time:

1 of 6 ∧ ∨

2 Enter the Channel number, Frequency, Date, Start time, Stop time, Keep and Quality settings, then click Record

Keywords

You can set recordings based on keywords including Actors name, Directors name, Movie or Program title and even Generic words.

1 Select Keyword from the Add Recording menu

2 Select the Keyword search type and enter your search parameters and then select one of the results

3 Select Record to record every instance of the selected keyword

Scheduled Recordings

If you want to see what shows you have scheduled to record you can do so by selecting the Scheduled option from the Recorded TV menu. From here you can also change the priority of recordings if there is a recording conflict and even see what you have recorded in the past.

1   Select Recorded TV from the TV + Movies menu

2   Select View Scheduled

You can sort the list by either date or show title and you can select a show from the list to see more information about it.

3   Select Series to display the list of series that are scheduled

...cont'd

You can see all the scheduled shows listed in the priority that
Windows Media Center will record them. This is important
should there be a conflict and multiple shows are on at the same
time. You can set what your priorities are from here.

4 Select Change Priorities

5 Using the arrows, change the priority order of the shows
and then click Done to return

Recording History

The History option provides you with a list of all scheduled
recordings that have gone past the schedule time, along with
status information on the recording (such as canceled, partial, etc).

1 Select History from the Scheduled menu

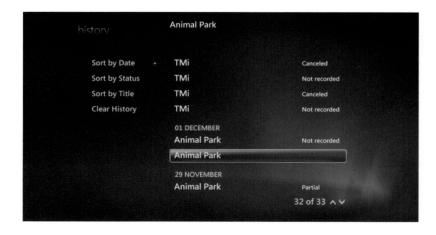

Searching

Now that you have access to 14 days worth of program information, thanks to the Guide, you can easily find what you are looking for by using the Search function. You can search by title, keyword and even by categories. You can then find out more information on what you find including any repeat showings. You can also then choose to watch or record it, if it is already airing or even set Windows Media Center to record it for you when it airs at a later time or day.

1 From the TV + Movies menu select Search

Don't forget

You can only search for items in the Guide that are within 14 days from the current date.

75

2 From the search menu select the menu item for the type of search you want to perform

Search Types

There are three main search types available to use:

- Title
- Keyword
- Categories

Searching by Title

This is by far the simplest search option – you just type in the title of what you are looking for and the results are displayed.

1 From the Title search option type the name of something you are searching for

2 Select the search result you are looking for (if available)

Searching by Keyword

This search option is used to find a show with the search word in either the show title, episode title or even a related show.

1 From the Keyword search option type something you are searching for

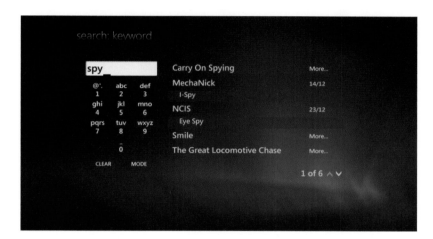

2 Select the search result you are looking for (if available)

Searching by Category

The final search option is the easiest one to use if you just want to find something to watch of a particular type – such as Drama.

The main categories that can be searched include:

- Film
- Drama
- Sports
- Children
- News

Each one of the 10 main categories has a number of sub-categories that can also be selected to fine tune your selection.

...cont'd

1 From the Categories search option select a category that is of interest to you

2 Select the sub-category that interests you or select All

3 Select one of the search results that interests you

If any of the selections are currently airing you can choose to watch them otherwise you have the option to record them later.

Playing DVDs

As long as you have a DVD player or recorder installed in your Windows Media Center computer you can play back DVDs.

1 Place the DVD you want to watch in your DVD drive

2 From the TV + Movies menu select Play DVD

3 The DVD will then start playing and you can use Windows Media Center as you would a DVD player

4 If you press the More button on the remote control you can see information about the chapter playing as well as the menu

Hot tip

If you are living in the US then you can also use one of the 200 disc mega-DVD changers from Sony or Niveus.

Hot tip

Windows Media Center now comes with a DVD decoder installed so you no longer have to buy one separately.

Don't forget

You can only play DVDs from the same region your Windows Media Center is from.

...cont'd

5 Select Movie Details from the menu to see more information about the DVD you are watching

Hot tip

You can change some of the playback functions on the remote control from the Settings menu.

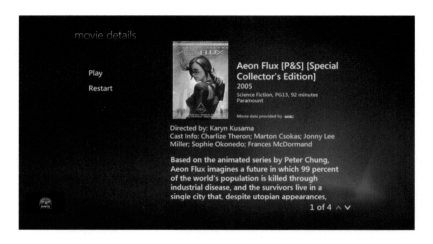

Parental Controls

If you have activated parental controls for DVD playback from the Settings menu and the DVD you are watching is in violation of those controls you will see the following message:

Don't forget

If you are using Parental Controls to stop certain content from being viewed, make sure the code you set to override the Parental Controls is not easy to guess.

1 Press the OK button and enter your 4 digit code

6 Music and Radio

This chapter will tell you everything you need to know about the various Music and Radio features of Windows Media Center including how to listen to the Radio, listen to your CDs and even how to add your CDs to the Music Library.

Music

Windows Media Center can be used as your own personal music jukebox. You can listen to music from CDs or from music stored on your Windows Media Center computer itself from within the Music Library.

You can also copy your CDs to your Music Library so that you can listen to them whenever you want, without the need for the CD to be in the computer.

You can view information about the tracks, albums and artists, cue up music to listen to, view your music in a number of different ways and even buy music online if you so wish. You can also easily search for your favorite tracks or artists and then listen to that track you may not have heard for a while.

Listen to all your music

If you are in a rush, or you just don't mind what you listen to, you can have Windows Media Center cue up all your music and just play everything for you.

Don't forget

If you want to buy music online, your Windows Media Center computer will need to be connected to the Internet.

1 From the Music menu, select Play All

Launching the Music Library

1 Select Music Library from the Music menu

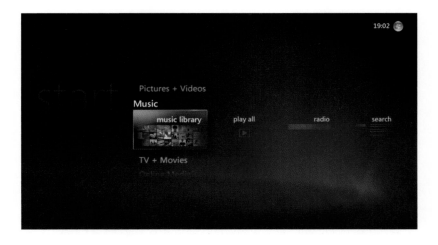

Music Library Views

Rather than just see your music as a list, there are a number of different views that you can use to sort your music and display it in useful ways.

Display by Album Artist
When selected, this view groups the albums by artist and shows you a thumbnail of the album cover to select from.

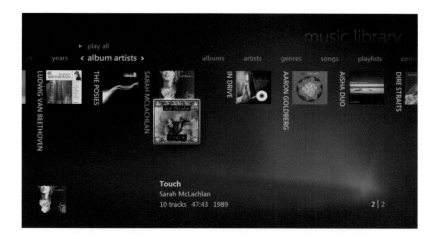

Display by Years
When selected, this view groups all your music together by the year it was released which can be really fun for listening to music from a time that may have special meaning for you, or just music you have not heard for a while.

Hot tip

Have a look at all the different views and find the one that suits you the best. These views can be changed easily so just work your way through them until you find one that you like.

Hot tip

If you have a large number of albums stored in your music library, setting the best view is very important to easily find what you are looking for.

Hot tip

On a number of the views, you can also choose between small thumbnails and normal size thumbnails, as well as just a plain text list.

Listening to a CD

Your Windows Media Center computer can be used as a CD player if you want it to be and you can listen to any of your CDs and even copy them to your media library to listen to again later.

Hot tip

If the CD does not play automatically, if you are given the option, select always have Windows Media Center play the CD. This option will be displayed by Windows Vista rather than by Windows Media Center.

1 Put the CD you want to listen to into the CD or DVD drive of your Windows Media Center computer

2 The CD should automatically start playing

If the CD does not play automatically, you can play it from within the music library.

3 Select Music Library from the Music menu

4 Select the album from the available list (it will be the one with the icon of a CD in the corner)

Don't forget

In order to see the CD icon, you will need to be on a view that shows the album cover thumbnails.

5 Select the Play Album button to play the entire album or

6 Click on a specific track title and then click Play Song

Don't forget

You will need to be connected to the Internet and have allowed Windows Media Center to automatically retrieve information on your music in order to see the album and track details, plus the artwork.

You will also have seen another button called Buy Music on some of the menus. If you click this it will connect to the Internet and give you the option of purchasing more music.

CD Ripping Options

Windows Media Center does not perform the actual ripping of tracks from a CD, Windows Media Player does. As such, any configuration settings that you want to change, specifically the type of audio file created and the bitrate used, needs to be changed from within Windows Media Player.

1 Launch Windows Media Player by clicking on the Start button and selecting Windows Media Player from the All Programs list

Hot tip

If you would like to hear demos of some of the different audio settings go to http://www. microsoft.com/windows/ windowsmedia/demos/ audio_quality_demos. aspx and have a listen for yourself.

2 Click on the arrow below the Rip button to display the options menu

3 Click on the More Options button

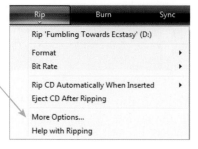

There are a number of different formats that can be used to rip the music to, including:

● MP3

● WAV

● Various Windows Media Audio formats

④ Choose the format you want the tracks to be ripped to

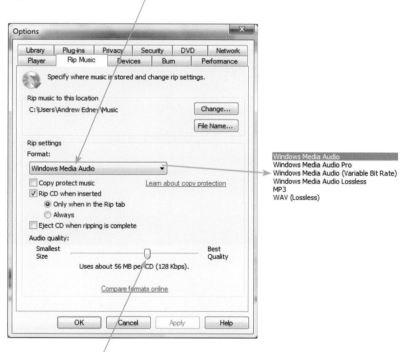

⑤ Use the slide bar to change the audio quality setting

⑥ Click Apply then OK

Ripping CDs in Windows Media Player

You can also choose to rip your CDs to your music library from within Windows Media Player instead of from Windows Media Center if you so wish. Just select the Rip option when the CD is in the drive to start the rip.

Hot tip

If you plan on synchronizing your music with any type of device at a later stage, you might want to consider selecting MP3 as your chosen format for the greatest device compatibility.

Don't forget

The higher the quality of the audio file, the more storage space is used.

Don't forget

If you do use Windows Media Player to rip your CDs, make sure you have added the folder that it rips to as a watched folder in Windows Media Center, otherwise you will not see the content.

Adding a CD to the Library

Now that you have listened to a CD, you may want to add it to your music library so that you can listen to it at any time without the need to have the CD available.

Setting Copy Options

The first time you try to copy a CD to your music library you will be presented with a couple of copy options.

1 Select whether or not you want to add copy protection to the music you are copying from CD to your music library then click Next to continue

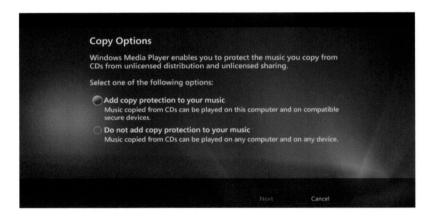

2 Check the box and click Next then Finish

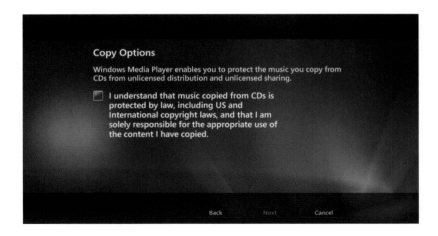

Copying a CD

1 From the Now Playing screen, click on Copy CD

Hot tip

If you have already added the CD to your music library, Windows Media Center will tell you it is already there and will not copy it for a second time.

2 Click on Yes to confirm you want to copy the CD

Hot tip

You can see the progress of the copy – a tick represents a completed copy and the spinning CD icon represents the track that is currently being copied.

3 When the copy has completed, click OK

Editing Information

There will be times when the information about the track or the album will not be found or may not be correct.

Unknown Album (07/12/2006 19:12:30)
Unknown Artist
12 tracks

You can edit any of the information, including the album or track title and the artist.

1   Select the track or album and press the More button on the remote control

Play
Add to Queue
Edit
Delete
Library Setup
Settings

2   Select Edit from the menu

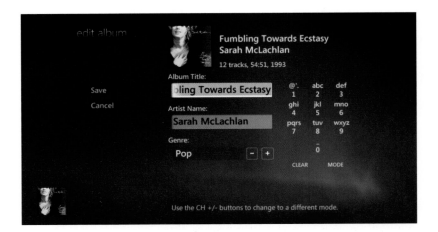

edit album   Fumbling Towards Ecstasy
Sarah McLachlan
12 tracks, 54:51, 1993

Album Title:
bling Towards Ecstasy

Save
Cancel

Artist Name:
Sarah McLachlan

Genre:
Pop   − +

@'.   abc   def
1   2   3
ghi   jkl   mno
4   5   6
pqrs   tuv   wxyz
7   8   9
−
0
CLEAR   MODE

Use the CH +/- buttons to change to a different mode.

3   Update the information as required using either your remote control keypad or a keyboard

4   Click Save

5   Repeat steps 1 through 4 for each track or album you wish to edit

Library Options

There are a number of different options available from within the Music Library when you press the More button on the remote control or you click the right mouse button when you have selected something from the library.

These options include:

- Play (which will play either the track or album)
- Add to Queue
- Burn (which will start the CD burning process)
- View Small (which will display a very small thumbnail view)
- View List (which changes the display to be a text list)
- Settings (which will launch the settings menu)

Hot tip

Deleting music from your music library, that you no longer listen to, frees up valuable storage space and gives you more room for music you do want to listen to.

Deleting Music

If you decide you no longer want to keep a track or an album, you can easily delete it from your music library.

1. Select the album or track

2. Press More and select Delete

   CONFIRM DELETE
   Are you sure you want to permanently delete the album Realize from the computer?
   | Yes | No |

3. Select Yes to confirm that you want to delete it from your computer

Hot tip

If you accidently delete a track or album, you might be able to get it back from the Recycle Bin on your desktop, by selecting the item and choosing Restore this item from the menu.

Queues and Playlists

A queue is described as a temporary list of tracks that you want to play and listen to. The advantage to using a queue is that you can select a large number of tracks and then let them play, rather than keep selecting tracks or albums each time you want to listen to something.

Adding to a Queue

1 Select the track or album you want to add to the queue and press the More button on your remote control

2 Select Add to Queue from the menu

3 Repeat steps 1 and 2 for all the music you want to add to the queue

4 Select the thumbnail in the bottom left corner of the screen to view the current queue

Hot tip

To make listening to the music more enjoyable, select the Shuffle mode so that the tracks are played in a random order. This can make it fun as you won't know what will be played next.

Editing a Queue

Once you have a queue of music playing you can edit the queue, including changing the sequence of the music or even removing tracks from the queue you no longer want to listen to.

1 Select Edit Queue

② Change the sequence of the tracks by pressing the up and down arrows on the screen

③ If you want to remove a track from the playlist, click on the X button

④ Select Done when you have finished

Playlists

Because a queue of music is temporary it will be deleted when you have finished with it, so if you really like the list of music you have put together in the queue you can save it as a playlist so that you can easily listen to it again later.

① Ensure your Queue contains all the tracks you want to save as part of a new playlist

② From the Queue, select Save as Playlist

③ Using the keypad on the remote control or a keyboard enter a name for your playlist

④ Click Save to complete the playlist creation process

Don't forget

Removing a track from the playlist does not delete it from your music library.

Hot tip

Playlists are great for quickly and easily listening to some of your favorite music. Create playlists for different moods so that you can listen to something particular depending on your mood.

...cont'd

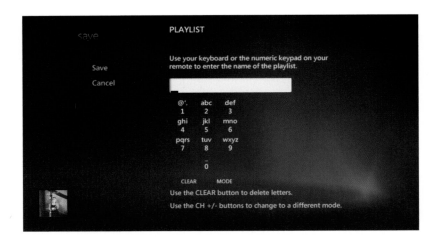

Selecting a Playlist

You can create as many playlists as you like. Selecting a playlist to listen to is very easy.

1 From the main Music Library screen change your library view to Playlists

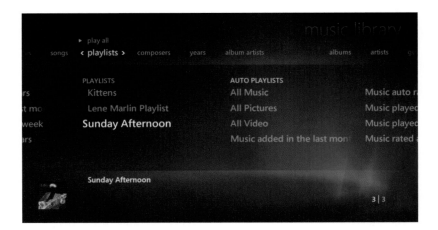

2 Scroll through the list of available playlists and select the one you want to listen to

3 Select Play to start listening to the chosen playlist

Now Playing

When you are listening to either a CD, a playlist or just music from your music library, an additional menu item appears called Now Playing + Queue. This new menu item can be used to quickly see what you are currently listening to and what is currently queued up, if you have been elsewhere within Windows Media Center looking at or doing something else.

1 From the Windows Media Center menu scroll to Now Playing + Queue and select Music

Hot tip

You can also see what other media is playing, such as DVDs, Videos or TV programs, from the Now Playing + Queue menu and then select it if you wish.

2 From here you can select View Queue to see what other music is waiting to be played or you can choose any of the other options

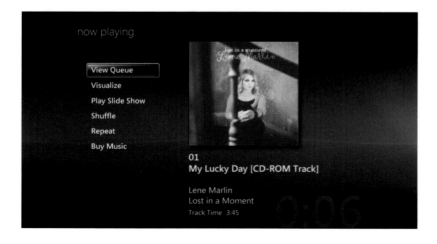

Hot tip

If you are listening to music from a CD, you will also see a button on the menu called Copy CD, which you can use to rip the CD, instead of going through the Music Library menu.

Searching

If you have a large music collection stored in your music library, it can sometimes be quite time consuming to find that one particular track or artist that you want to listen to.

This is where the search function plays a vital role. You can use it to search for any track, artist, album or genre.

1 From the Music menu, select Search

2 Using either the keypad on your remote control or the keyboard, enter some text for what you are searching for (as you type the results will appear)

Hot tip

You don't need to enter the full details of what you are searching for, just a part of a track title or artist is sufficient. Even a search for Pop will display all tracks with the genre set as Pop.

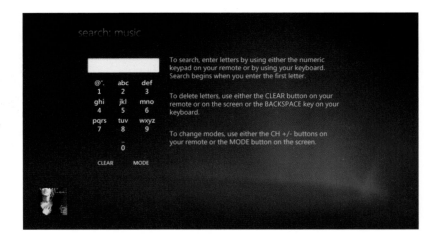

3 If the results contain the music you are looking for just highlight and select it

 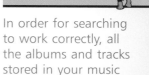
4 You can then choose a particular album or track from the selection, add the selections to the queue or even choose to play all the tracks from the selection

5 Repeat steps 1 through 4 for any other music you want to search for

Radio

The Radio button allows you to listen to FM radio stations and also allows you to create presets for your favorite stations.

Don't forget

You need to have an FM tuner installed in your Windows Media Center computer in order to listen to FM radio stations.

 From the Music menu, select Radio

Beware

If you have two tuners installed that support FM Radio you must ensure that each tuner is connected to its own FM radio signal source. This is because Windows Media Center will use the first available tuners as they are needed and if that tuner does not have an FM radio signal then you will not be able to listen to Radio.

Don't forget

Windows Media Center will have problems picking up a radio source if the signal is too weak.

2 Click on the FM Radio button

3 If you know the frequency of the radio station you want to listen to enter it using either a keyboard or the keypad on the remote control or

Use Seek to quickly search for a usable signal and Tune if you want to fine tune the signal.

4 Click on the Seek or Tune - and + buttons until you find the radio station you want to listen to

Saving as a Preset Radio Station

You can also save the radio station as a preset so that you can just click the preset in order to listen to it again.

1 Click the Save as Preset button

Beware

Certain Tuner hardware cannot receive both an FM radio signal and a TV signal at the same time. Check with the manufacturer of the tuner to confirm this. TV takes priority over Radio and Radio will stop if you have a scheduled TV program to record.

2 Enter a name for the radio station and click Save

...cont'd

Hot tip

If you want to hear something again that was just said on the radio you can press the REPLAY button on the remote control to skip back 7 seconds.

Hot tip

You can also listen to Internet Radio. To do this you need to install a partner application via the Program Library.

Hot tip

The last radio station you listened to should appear on the Music menu as well.

Playing a Preset Radio Station

Now that you have added a preset radio station, or a number of presets, it is very easy to listen to them whenever you want.

1 Select Radio from the Music menu

2 Scroll to the presets option near the top of the screen

3 Select the preset radio station you want to listen to

4 If you need to adjust the tuning, click Edit Preset or use the - and + buttons as necessary

7 Pictures and Videos

This chapter will tell you about the Picture and Video library, including how to setup a slideshow.

Picture Library

The Picture Library is the place to store all of your pictures so that you can view them and show them to your friends on your television rather than just on your computer.

From the Picture Library you can:

● View individual pictures or a number of pictures as a slide show

● Sort your pictures by name, date taken or even using tags

● Edit your pictures

● Print your pictures

 From the Pictures + Videos menu select Picture Library

Once you have entered the picture library, you will see all of your available pictures and folders presented initially in the folders view. This folder view shows a few thumbnail images of the contents of the folder along with the name of the folder, its creation date and also the number of items within the folder.

The other views that are available for you to select are:

● Tags (which is a new feature for Windows Media Center)

● Date Taken

...cont'd

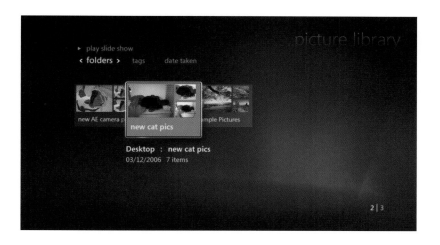

Hot tip

When viewing a single picture you can zoom in on the picture by pressing the OK button on your remote control or Enter on the keyboard.

2 Select a folder to view its contents

Hot tip

You can customize the slide show from the Settings option on the Tasks menu or by selecting Settings after pressing the More button on the remote control.

From here you can select an individual picture to view or even play a slide show of all of the pictures in that particular folder.

Playing a Slide Show

If you want to play a slide show of your pictures instead of looking at each one individually, all you have to do is select the Play Slide Show button and sit back and relax.

Hot tip

Windows Media Center will display your pictures in High Definition (if your display supports it) during a slide show. This is a change from previous versions of Media Center which used to "down sample" the pictures.

Tags

Tags is a new feature that is introduced with the Windows Photo Gallery as a cool way of organizing your photo collections. Tags can be used by Windows Media Center to display photos for you. This works by assigning a keyword to individual pictures or to collections of pictures.

Tagging Pictures

The assigning of tags to pictures is performed in Windows Photo Gallery.

Hot tip

When you tag pictures, they can be stored in a variety of different places but when you select that tag to view them, they will appear as though they are stored together.

1 Click the Start button then All Programs and then click on Windows Photo Gallery

2 Select the picture you want to assign a tag to

3 Click the right mouse button to reveal the menu and select Add Tags to launch the Info pane

You can also display the Info pane by clicking on Info on the toolbar.

4 Type a tag into the box that is under the select picture

5 You can also drag the picture to the appropriate tag in the Navigation pane

Viewing Tagged Pictures

Once you have tagged all of your pictures it is very easy to view them in Windows Media Center.

1 From the Picture Library select the Tags view

2 Select the tag folder that you want to view

Hot tip

You can add as many tags as you want to each picture.

Hot tip

You can also rate your pictures out of 5 stars so that you can search for certain ratings later.

Beware

Pictures that you have added Tags to may take a short while before they appear tagged in Windows Media Center.

105

Editing Pictures

You can use Windows Media Center to do some very basic editing of the pictures you have stored in your picture library.

 Select the picture you want to edit from the picture library and press the More button on the remote control

 Select Picture Details from the menu

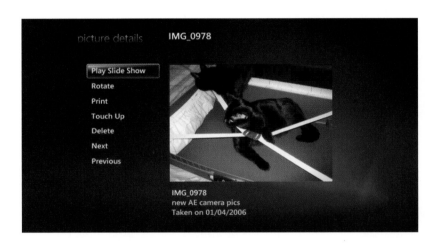

Rotating a Picture

You can rotate the picture clockwise 90 degrees.

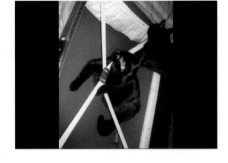

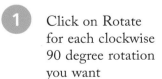 Click on Rotate for each clockwise 90 degree rotation you want

Printing a Picture

You can print a picture directly to your printer from here as well.

 Click on the Print button

Touching Up Pictures

You can perform minor touch ups on your pictures from within Windows Media Center, including adjusting the Red Eye, the Contrast and even resizing a picture using the Crop function.

1 Click on Touch Up

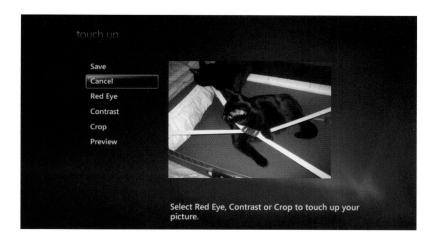

Hot tip

If you want to do anything but the very basic editing of pictures, it is highly recommended you invest in a product designed specifically for this purpose, or see if the Windows Photo Gallery is sufficient for your needs.

2 Click on the Red Eye button and/or the Contrast button to adjust the settings

3 Click on the Crop button and then use the arrow buttons and the magnifier buttons to select what you want to crop

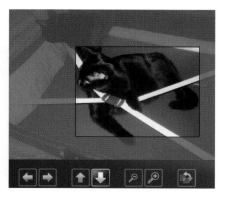

Beware

Some of the changes might be so minor that you may not even notice the difference between the edited picture and the original picture.

4 Click on Preview to see the finished result

5 Click on Save when you have finished editing the picture

Video Library

Very similar to the Pictures Library, the Video Library contains all of your movies, whether they are from your camcorder or ones that you have downloaded from the Internet. As long as they are stored on your Windows Media Center computer you can access them from here.

 From the Pictures + Videos menu select Video Library

Don't forget

Recorded TV programs are not stored in your Video Library.

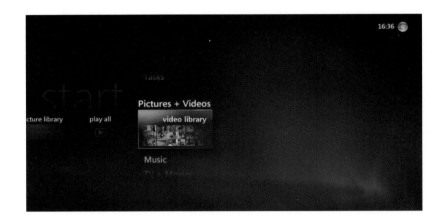

Don't forget

In order to see your videos you must have Windows Media Center watching any folders that contain videos.

108

Once you have entered the video library, you will see all of your available videos and folders presented initially in the folders view. This folder view shows a few thumbnail images of the contents of the folder along with the name of the folder, its creation date and also the number of items within the folder.

Don't forget

You may need to install additional codecs in order to play back some of the videos correctly.

...cont'd

You can also view the contents of your video library by date taken.

2   Select a video file or a folder containing videos

Hot tip

Another new feature in Windows Media Center is the ability to view related files if they are in the same folder, for example movie files stored in the same folder as your pictures. You can do this whenever you see the related option displayed in a folder.

You will then be presented with a thumbnail view of the contents of the chosen folder. Again, you can also view the contents by date.

3   Select a video to begin playback

4   You can also look at information on the video by pressing the More button on the remote control and selecting Video Details

Beware

Not all videos will support the ability to fast forward or rewind.

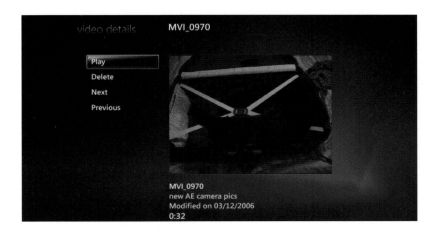

Hot tip

You can even burn your videos to a CD or DVD from here instead of going through the Burn CD/DVD option on the Tasks menu.

Supported File Types

Windows Media Center supports a number of different file types for both pictures and video.

Supported Picture Files

Picture File Types (format)	File name extensions
Joint Photographic Experts Group	.jpg, .jpeg
Tagged Image File Format	.tif, .tiff
Graphics Interchange Format	.gif
Bitmap	.bmp
Windows Metafile	.wmf
Portable Network Graphics	.png

Supported Video Files

Video File Types (Format)	File name extensions
Windows Media	.wm, .asf
Windows Media Video	.wmv
Window video	.avi
Movie	.mpeg, .mpg, .mpe, .m1v, .mp2, .mpv2

8 CD/DVD Writing

This chapter will explain about each type of CD and DVD you can create and then guide you through the process of actually creating and burning them.

Creating CDs and DVDs

From within Windows Media Center, you have the ability to create and burn both CDs and DVDs with various content on them. The types of CDs and DVDs you can create includes:

- Audio CDs of your favorite music

- Data CDs to archive your files

- Video DVDs so that you can watch your favorite recordings on stand-alone DVD players and other computers

- Data DVDs to archive your larger files

- Slide Show DVDs so that you can watch your favorite pictures while listening to music on stand-alone DVD players and other computers as part of a slideshow

Windows Media Center supports the following types of media:

- CD-R

- CD-RW

- DVD-R

- DVD-RW

- DVD+R

- DVD+RW

Don't forget

Your DVD or CD recorder in your Windows Media Center computer will need to support the type of media you want to use to make your recordings.

1 From the Tasks menu, select Burn CD/DVD

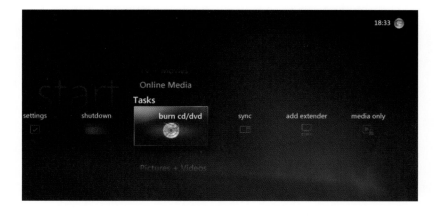

Windows Media Center comes with the Sonic Burn CD/DVD application preinstalled. You can add other applications, such as Nero if you want. Any installed applications with CD or DVD writing capabilities should appear here.

2 If you have any other CD or DVD writing applications installed, ignore them and select Sonic Burn CD/DVD

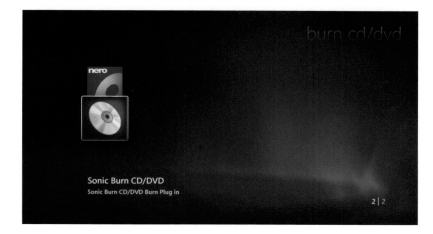

3 Insert either a writable CD or DVD (depending on what you want to create and write) into your CD or DVD recorder and click Retry

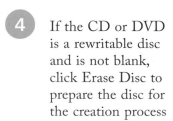

INSERT MEDIA

Please insert writeable media that is compatible with your CD or DVD recorder, and then select Retry.

Retry Cancel

4 If the CD or DVD is a rewritable disc and is not blank, click Erase Disc to prepare the disc for the creation process

ERASE DISC?

To burn a disc in this format, all files must first be erased from the disc. What do you want to do?

Erase Disc Cancel

Data DVDs

Data DVDs contain files that are written to DVD so that they can be used in other computers or for archiving some of your files.

1 From the Select Disc Format screen select Data DVD and click Next

2 Enter a name for the DVD and click Next

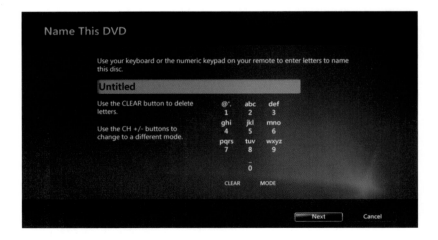

3 Select the location to browse for the media you want to add to the DVD and click Next

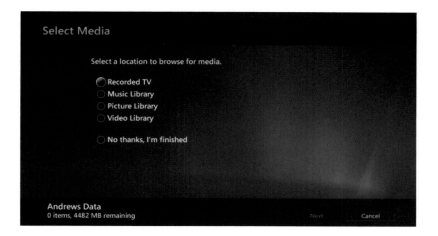

4 Select the media you want to add (for example a television program you recorded that is available in Recorded TV) and click Next

Beware

Some media content might be copy protected. While you will be able to write this content to a Data DVD, you may not be able to play it back.

5 If you want to add additional media to the DVD select Add More

From the Review & Edit List, you can change the name of the DVD and remove items from the list prior to burning the DVD or even clear the entire list if you want to start all over again.

...cont'd

6 Select another location from the Select Media screen and add any additional files

Beware

Keep an eye on the amount of free space available on your DVD.

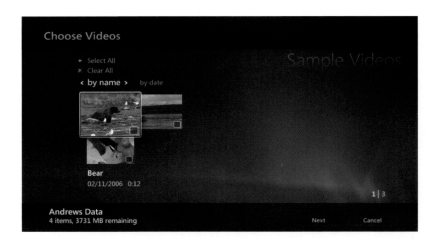

7 Repeat steps 5 and 6 until you have added all the files you want to the list

8 Go through the list of items on the Review and Edit List screen and confirm you have added all the files you want

9 Select Burn DVD   **Burn DVD**

Burning the Disc

The final step in the process is actually burning your disc.

1 Select Yes to begin the process of burning the disc

2 When you see the Burn Progress dialog box, click OK to continue or

3 If you need to stop the burning, click Stop

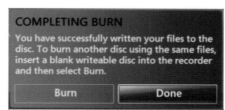

4 After the burn has completed click Done or

5 If you want to burn another copy of the same disc, click Burn

6 Check that the files have written correctly to the disc

7 If there are any errors try rewriting using a different disc

Hot tip

This process is the same for whichever type of disc you are writing in whatever format you choose to use.

Beware

Even though you can choose to continue to use Windows Media Center while the burning is taking place, it is advisable not to.

Hot tip

If you have written a Data DVD you can use Windows Vista to check the contents. If you have written a Video DVD try playing the DVD in your DVD player.

DVD Slide Shows

The DVD Slide Show option allows you to create a DVD of your favorite pictures and have them played to your favorite piece or pieces of music. The DVD can then be played back in any DVD player that supports the type of DVD you have written to.

The way this works is that the pictures are converted into an MPEG-2 video file and the music encoded into Dolby Digital audio giving the best possible quality of both sound and picture.

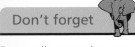

Don't forget

Depending on the type of DVD you are using, you may be asked to erase it first.

1. Ensure a recordable DVD is inserted in your DVD drive

2. Select Burn CD/DVD from the Tasks menu

3. If you have more than one program listed, choose Sonic Burn CD/DVD

4. Select DVD Slide Show from the Select Disc Format options and click Next

5. Enter a name for the DVD Slide Show, for example Andrews Slides, and then click Next

6. Select Music Library from the Select Media screen and click Next to continue

Beware

You can add 999 items to your DVD, however you must remember that the 999 items includes both pictures and music.

Hot tip

You can add all of your music from your library by clicking on Select All.

7 Select the music you want to listen to while watching the slides, then click Next

8 On the Review & Edit List screen, click Add More

9 Select Picture Library and click Next

10 Select the pictures you want as part of your slide show and then click Next

11 Select Burn DVD, then Yes to burn the disc with the files

Hot tip

As each picture will be displayed for only 7 seconds, make sure you add enough music to last for the whole of your slide show.

Hot tip

The pictures are displayed in the order that they are added to the DVD and the music plays in the order it is added as well, so make sure you change the sequence to the order you want before burning the DVD.

Video DVDs

If you want to be able to play back some of your recorded media content on a stand-alone DVD player, you can use the Video DVD option to create and burn a DVD for that very purpose.

1 From the Select Disc Format screen select Video DVD and click Next

2 Enter a name for the Video DVD and click Next

3 Select either Recorded TV (if you want to select programs you have recorded) or Video Library (if you want to select videos you may have added yourself) then click Next

Beware

Some media content might be copy protected. While you will be able to write this content to a Video DVD, you may not be able to play it back.

4 Select the TV program or video you want to add to the DVD so that a tick appears in the box for each one then click Next

Beware

Burning a Video DVD can take a considerable amount of time because the media files are also being converted into a format that your DVD player can playback.

5 If you want to add additional media click Add More and repeat steps 3 and 4

6 Click Burn DVD and then click Yes to initiate the copy

7 After the burning has completed, test the DVD in a stand-alone DVD player to make sure it works correctly

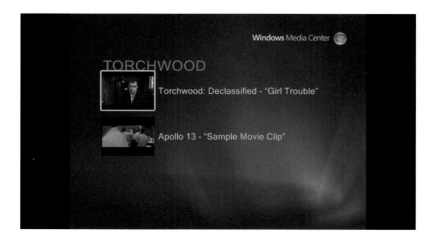

Don't forget

You cannot change the layout or what is displayed on the DVD menu. If you need to do this then you will need to use a different authoring package.

Audio CDs

You can create audio CDs of your favorite music that can be played back on most CD players both in the home and in the car.

Various types of digital audio files are supported for audio CD writing, including:

Beware

Audio files that have been copy protected will not be able to be written to the audio CD.

- MP3s

- Windows Media Audio (WMA)

- WAV files

During the audio CD creation process, the various audio files are converted into a format that CD players can playback.

1 Select Audio CD and click Next to continue

Select Disc Format

    Audio CD
    Data CD

Select this format if you want to play the CD in a CD player.

2 Enter a name for the audio CD and click Next to continue

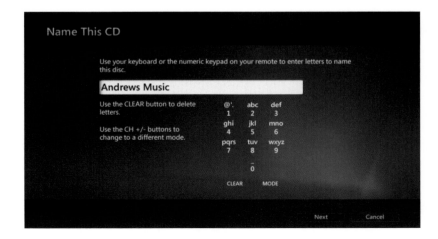

Name This CD

Use your keyboard or the numeric keypad on your remote to enter letters to name this disc.

Andrews Music

Use the CLEAR button to delete letters.

Use the CH +/- buttons to change to a different mode.

@'.	abc	def
1	2	3
ghi	jkl	mno
4	5	6
pqrs	tuv	wxyz
7	8	9
	0	
CLEAR	MODE	

Next   Cancel

3 Select the music you want to add to the audio CD by choosing from the available music and selecting the album cover and then the individual songs or pieces of music, then click Next

Hot tip

The amount of time remaining on the CD is shown in the bottom left corner of each screen and is updated each time you add music to the list.

4 If you want to add some additional music to the CD, click Add More and repeat step 3

Hot tip

You can change the sequence in which the music will be played by using the arrows to move individual songs, or even the X button to remove the song entirely from the list.

5 Select Burn CD and then click Yes to initiate the burning process, then click Done when the CD has finished

123

Other Burning Applications

You don't have to use the preinstalled Sonic application if you don't want to. There are plenty of other applications you can use, for example Nero.

Nero gives you a couple of additional formats over the Sonic application, specifically:

- Video CDs
- VCD Slide Shows

1 Select Burn CD/DVD from the Tasks menu

2 Select Nero Burn (or another application)

3 Select the format of the disc you want to create and then click Next to continue

Select Disc Format

○ Audio CD
○ Data CD
○ Video CD
○ VCD Slide Show

Select this format if you want to play the CD in a CD player.

Next   Cancel

4 Add the media content as before

5 Burn the disc and then test it to make sure it works

Windows Vista also comes preinstalled with Windows DVD Maker, which you can use to create DVDs of your videos and digital photos. You can launch Windows DVD Maker from Start, then All Programs and then selecting Windows DVD Maker.

9 Online Media & Tasks

This chapter will guide you through the Online Media menu and also how to synchronize your content to a portable media device.

Online Media

The Online Media functionality is designed specifically to deliver entertainment, such as games and movies on-demand, over a broadband connection direct to your Windows Media Center computer.

Movie studios and other major content providers will be delivering content through Online Media. Some of this content will be free and some of it will require a subscription, depending on what the content is.

Program Library

The Program Library is currently the only menu item available with Windows Media Center "out of the box".

Any Windows Media Center compatible programs that are installed will appear in the Program Library and be easily launched from the comfort of your armchair.

 Select Program Library from the Online Media menu

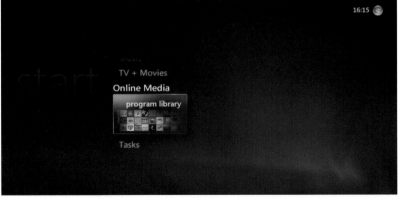

From here you will be able to see all available programs as the default view shows the programs by name. You can also choose to filter the programs and only view programs related to:

● TV and Movies

● Music and Radio

● Pictures

- News and Sports
- Games
- Lifestyle
- Tasks

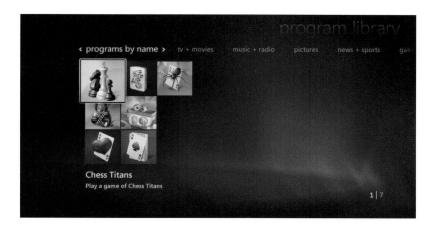

You can easily filter the view by clicking on the remote control until programs by name is selected, then using the left and right buttons to scroll through the available views.

Initially, the only programs that are available are a number of games, such as Chess Titans and Freecell. These games have been specifically designed to be played on the Windows Media Center.

2 Select a game you want to play

Information about the game will be displayed at the bottom of the screen when you highlight it.

Program Library

Adding to the Start Menu

You can even add your favorite game or application to the start menu so that it appears in the Online Media menu.

1 Select Program Library from the Online Media menu

2 Highlight the game or application you want to add and then press the More button on the remote control

Hot tip

When added to the Start menu, the program will appear in the associated category. For example, if it is TV related, it will appear on the TV menu.

3 Select Add to Start Menu

4 Select Yes to confirm that you want to add the selected application to the Start menu under Online Media

Hot tip

You can even sort the programs by date or by most used to make it easier to find what you are looking for.

You will then see that program shown in the Online Media menu. You can launch it by simply selecting it instead of going through the program library menu.

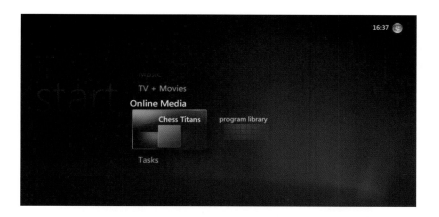

Hot tip

You can easily replace a program on the start menu by choosing another available program and select Add to Start Menu.

Removing from the Start Menu

If you want to remove that program from the Start menu:

① Press the More button on the remote control while highlighting the program in the program library

② Select Remove from Start Menu

Don't forget

Selecting Hide on a program does not delete it, it only hides it.

Hiding a Program

You can hide a program so that it no longer appears in the program library.

① Right click on the program in the program library

② Select Hide

③ Select Yes to confirm

If you want to add it back again you will need to do this through the Program Library settings menu which can be found within the General Settings under Tasks, Settings.

Hot tip

You can also change the settings for the Program Library by selecting Settings then press the More button on the remote control or click the right mouse button on any program.

Sync to Device

There are a number of portable Media Center devices available on the market. These devices are small, portable hand-held systems and are designed to enable you to take your media with you wherever you go.

Hot tip

Any Portable Media Center device that is designed to work with Media Center 2005 should work with Windows Media Center.

Hot tip

Ensure any drivers that are required to use the portable media device are installed and configured.

Hot tip

If you see an error message telling you that there was no device detected, check that the cable connecting your device is attached correctly and that the device is switched on.

① Connect your portable Media Center device to your Windows Media Center computer

② Select Sync from the Tasks menu

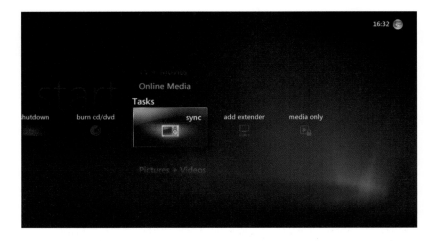

3 If your device is already synchronized with another computer, select Yes to create a new synchronization

SYNC TO DEVICE
This device is already synchronized with another computer. Do you want to create a new synchronization and replace the previous one?

Yes   No

Beware

If you select Yes to create a new synchronization, then your old one is deleted, so if you want to use your device with another Media Center you will need to re-synchronize the device.

4 From the manage list, select Add More

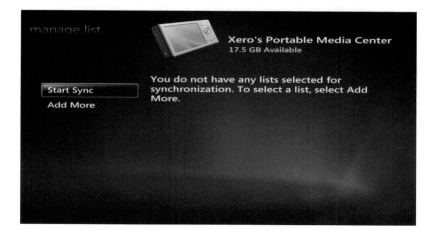

manage list

Xero's Portable Media Center
17.5 GB Available

Start Sync
Add More

You do not have any lists selected for synchronization. To select a list, select Add More.

Hot tip

The name of the portable device and the amount of free space is always shown at the top of each screen so you always know how much room you have left on the device.

131

5 Select the type of content you want to synchronize to the portable device

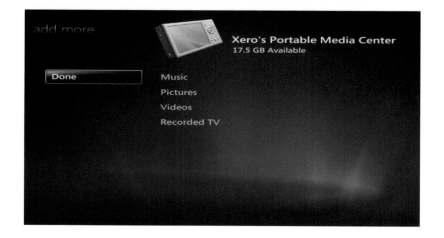

add more

Xero's Portable Media Center
17.5 GB Available

Done

Music
Pictures
Videos
Recorded TV

Synchronizing Content

You can choose to synchronize Music, Pictures, Videos and Recorded TV to your portable Media Center device.

1 From the chosen content type, check the box for any available content to be added to the synchronization list

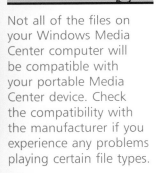

Beware

Not all of the files on your Windows Media Center computer will be compatible with your portable Media Center device. Check the compatibility with the manufacturer if you experience any problems playing certain file types.

2 Click on Save when you have selected all the content you want

3 If you want to add more content, select Add More and then select the relevant content type and add whatever you want, as before

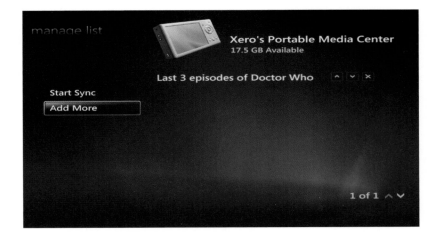

4 If you want to add some of your Music, select Music from the Add More menu

5 Check the box for whichever music you want to add to the synchronization list

6 Click Save to return to the manage list screen

Synchronizing Pictures

Unlike all the other content you can synchronize, in order to synchronize Pictures from your Windows Media Center, you must first create a pictures playlist in Windows Media Player.

If you have not yet created any picture playlists in Windows Media Player, you will be advised that there are no playlists.

1 Launch Windows Media Player to create a new playlist

Hot tip

In order to save time, set up your picture playlists before you start the synchronization steps.

...cont'd

2 Click Library and then click Create Playlist

3 Enter a name for your picture playlist

Hot tip

Double-click on the new picture playlist to play it using Windows Media Player so that you can check that the pictures you have added are correct and are all there.

4 Select the pictures you want to add to the new playlist

5 Drag them to the Drag items here box to add them to the new playlist

6 Back in Windows Media Center select Pictures from the Add More menu

7 Check the box for the picture playlist you want to add

8 Click Save to return to the manage list screen

Starting a Synchronization

Now that you have added all the content you wish to synchronize to your list, the final stage is actually performing the synchronization itself.

1 From the manage list screen, select Start Sync

Hot tip

If you want to remove something from the list before starting the synchronization, just click on the X button.

2 The synchronization will then start. If you need to stop it click Stop at anytime or click OK to continue using Windows Media Center

Beware

If you choose to edit the synchronization lists while the synchronization is in progress, you will most likely have to perform another synchronization to ensure all the selected content has been synchronized correctly.

3 When the synchronization has completed, click Done to finish the process

4 Check the portable device to see if the content is there

Media Only Mode

Media Only Mode is used to stop the Windows Media Center window from being closed without your permission, for example so that your children cannot gain access to Windows Vista in order to surf the Internet or watch movies using Windows Media Player, among other things.

When it is enabled, Windows Media Center remains in Full Screen Mode so that the window cannot be resized, moved or closed, and the Shut Down options are changed to only allow Log Off, Shut Down, Restart and Sleep.

1 From the Tasks menu, select media only

2 Select Yes to enter Media Only mode

3 To switch off Media Only Mode, select Exit Media Only from the Tasks menu

10 Media Center Extenders

This chapter will explain what a Media Center Extender is, how to setup and configure one and what they can do, along with some troubleshooting steps and assistance with network bandwidth monitoring.

What is an Extender?

Windows Media Center Extenders are devices that connect to your Windows Media Center computer and allow you to experience some of the great features of Windows Media Center in other rooms of your home, without the need to have a separate Windows Media Center computer there.

There are a number of different devices that are or can act as a Windows Media Center Extender. These devices are connected to your home network, either by a wired Ethernet connection or via Wireless.

Probably one of the easiest Extenders to use at the moment is the Microsoft Xbox 360 games console. Apart from being able to play games, it also has built-in Extender functionality and a very simple easy to use wizard for connecting to a Windows Media Center computer.

Beware

At it's release, Windows Media Center only supported the Microsoft Xbox 360 as an Extender. As time goes on, other devices will be supported. Take a look at http://www.microsoft.com/extender to keep up to date with which devices are supported.

138

Beware

It is very unlikely that the original Xbox will ever be supported as a Windows Media Center Extender.

What can it do?

Once connected to your Windows Media Center computer, you will be able to do a number of things, including:

- Listen to your music collection which you have stored on your Windows Media Center computer

- Browse your favorite photographs or watch a slide show, including playing music along with the show

- Play home movies or watch other videos, including those you may have downloaded from the Internet, as long as they are supported

● Watch or record your favorite TV shows (if you record any shows they are still stored on the Windows Media Center computer and not on your Xbox 360)

A really nice feature of the Windows Media Center Extenders is that each Extender can be doing something different to that of the Windows Media Center computer. For example, the person using the extender could be watching a recorded TV program while others are listening to the radio on the Windows Media Center computer itself.

Each extender has it's own Windows user account that is created during the configuration process. This account is unique to a particular extender and includes various settings relating to that extender, including information on the locations of media files.

Supported Audio and Video Formats

There are a number of supported audio and video formats that can be played from your Windows Media Center computer through your Windows Media Center Extender. These include:

Audio Format	Video Format
Windows Media Audio (WMA) Standard	MPEG-1 with MPEG audio
WMA Pro	MPEG-2 with MPEG audio or AC-3 audio
WMA Lossless	Windows Media Video (WMV) 7, 8, 9 with WMA Standard or WMA Pro audio
MP3	WMV Image 1 & 2 (Photo Story 1, 2 or 3)
Any other format that provides a DirectShow decoder	

Hot tip

You can connect as many as five different Media Center Extenders at one time, all performing different tasks.

Beware

The more Extenders you are using, the more network bandwidth is utilized and the greater the strain on the Windows Media Center computer.

Unavailable Features

There are a few features of Windows Media Center that are not available through the Media Center Extender.

These include:

WMC Feature	Features not available to the Extender
Pictures	Printing
	Transitions (animated and cross-fade)
Music	Visualizations
	Fast Forward or Rewind
	Listen to audio CDs on the Media Center
TV	Set Up TV Signal
	Adjust Display Settings
	Slow motion
	Step forward or backward
	Zoom
Videos	Fast Forward or Rewind (other then Recorded TV Shows)
	Watch DVDs from the Media Center
Settings	Music
	DVD
	Visual and Sound Effects
	Automatic Download Options
	Set Up TV Signal
	Configure Your TV or Monitor
	Remote Control Set Up
General & Privacy	Retrieve media information for CDs and DVDs from the Internet

Hot tip

If you do require some or all of this functionality in another room in your home, consider buying or building another Windows Media Center computer. Depending on what you want it to do, you could reduce the specification of the machine in order to keep the costs down.

Firewall Changes

During the setup and configuration of the Windows Media Center Extender, a number of changes are required to be made to the firewall on your Windows Media Center computer.

These include opening a number of ports and adding some exceptions in order to allow an Extender to connect securely across your home network to your Windows Media Center computer.

If you are using the Windows Firewall these changes are made automatically for you. If you are not using the Windows Firewall, or you are using multiple firewalls, you will need to make the changes manually.

Adding ports manually

The table below shows the port numbers, corresponding protocols and the scope for each addition that is required.

Port Number	Protocol	Scope
554	TCP	Local Subnet Only
1900	UDP	Local Subnet Only
2177	TCP	Local Subnet Only
2177	UDP	Local Subnet Only
3390	TCP	Local Subnet Only
5004 and 5005	UDP	Local Subnet Only
7777 - 7781	UDP	Local Subnet Only
8554 - 8558	TCP	Local Subnet Only
10244	TCP	Local Subnet Only
50004 - 50013	UDP	Local Subnet Only

For specific help in configuring certain types of firewalls, take a look at http://www.microsoft.com/windowsxp/mediacenter/extender/setup/default.mspx and select your firewall if it is listed.

Don't forget

If you are not using the Windows Firewall you will need to add these to the firewall you are using manually.

Beware

If you are adding these to your firewall manually, and you are not sure what you are doing, consult the manual that came with your firewall product before continuing. If you make a mistake the security of your network could be compromised.

Xbox 360 Setup

The process for connecting your Xbox 360 to your Windows Media Center involves steps on both devices. The following steps are to be performed on the Xbox 360.

1 Ensure the Xbox 360 is switched on and connected to your home network

Hot tip

Ensure you have downloaded and installed any software updates to your Xbox 360 before continuing. These updates can include enhancements and fixes and can be obtained by connecting to Xbox Live and if there are any available, just agreeing to the installation.

2 Move to the System blade and select Media Center

3 Select the Media Center button to continue

...cont'd

4 You may see a message relating to either network connections or wireless networks – if you do, just click on Continue

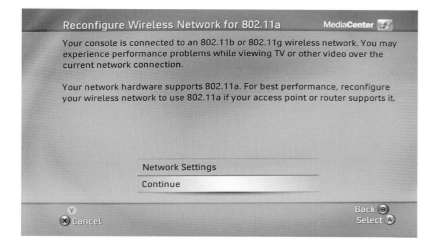

Reconfigure Wireless Network for 802.11a — MediaCenter

Your console is connected to an 802.11b or 802.11g wireless network. You may experience performance problems while viewing TV or other video over the current network connection.

Your network hardware supports 802.11a. For best performance, reconfigure your wireless network to use 802.11a if your access point or router supports it.

Network Settings
Continue

Y
X Cancel   Back B / Select A

Hot tip

If you are using wireless to connect your Xbox 360 to your home network, try to use 802.11a as it is much better suited to streaming TV and video than either 802.11b or 802.11g.

5 A Media Center Setup Key is then generated and displayed. Make sure you write this number down

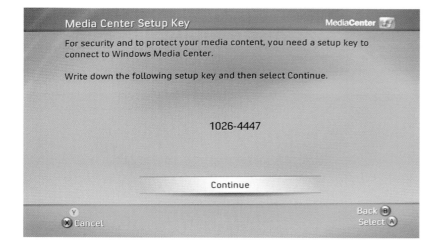

Media Center Setup Key — MediaCenter

For security and to protect your media content, you need a setup key to connect to Windows Media Center.

Write down the following setup key and then select Continue.

1026-4447

Continue

Y
X Cancel   Back B / Select A

Beware

At this point the screen displayed on your Xbox 360 will tell you to download and install software to your Media Center computer. You can safely ignore this as the software is already built into Windows Media Center and was only needed for Media Center 2005.

6 Click Continue to finish the setup process on the Xbox 360

Media Center Setup

Now that you have completed the steps on the Xbox 360, you must finish the setup on the Windows Media Center computer. The following steps are to be performed on the Windows Media Center computer.

Don't forget

Make sure your Windows Media Center computer is connected to your home network.

1 From the main menu, go to Tasks and select add extender

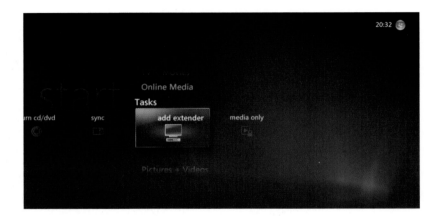

2 Select Next to get started

3 You will now need to enter the 8-digit Setup key that was generated on the Xbox 360, the one you wrote down, and click Next

Hot tip

Don't worry if you have forgotten the key or lost it, just go back to the Xbox 360 and press the B button on the controller to display the key again.

4   The Changing Computer Settings screen just advises you that certain changes will need to be made to the Windows Firewall settings and services, so just click Next to continue

5   Select Yes, you would like to enable Away Mode and click next to continue

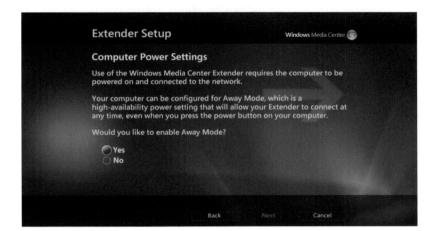

6   Select Yes (recommended), you do want to be able to see your media folders on your Extender, then click Next to continue the setup process

...cont'd

At this point, Windows Media Center completes the configuration, searches for the Extender and attempts to contact and configure the Extender. If you selected that you wanted to see your media files, these will be configured as well, along with the Away Mode setting. Finally, Windows Media Center will connect to the Extender.

Beware

A special users account is created to be used with the connection between the Extender and Windows Media Center computer, including permissions to those shared folders. Do not delete this account!

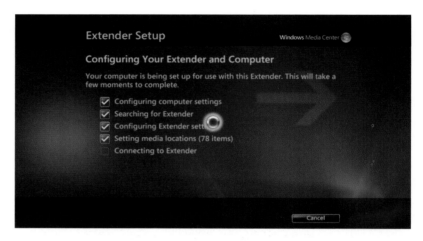

If everything is successful, you will notice that your Xbox 360 now displays the Windows Media Center main menu.

You will also see a You Are Done! screen displayed on your Windows Media Center.

7 Click Finish

You can now start using Windows Media Center through your Xbox 360.

When you have finished, you can close the connection by selecting close from the Tasks menu on the Xbox 360.

Launching Media Center

Once the initial setup and configuration has been completed, any time you want to launch Windows Media Center from the Xbox 360 console, just select Media Center from the Media blade and the Xbox 360 will connect to the Windows Media Center computer and display the main menu.

Hot tip

If your Xbox 360 is switched off and you press the START button on the Media Center remote control (also known as the Green Button), the Xbox 360 will switch on and automatically connect to Windows Media Center if it is available.

Adding Additional Extenders

Selecting the add extender menu option from Tasks is not the only way to add an extender.

For example, your Windows Media Center computer might automatically detect an extender on your network and prompt you as to whether or not you would like to set it up. Selecting Yes will launch the add extender wizard.

Hot tip

You can turn off the Windows Media Center notifications if you find them distracting. You can do this from the Tasks, settings, Extender, options menu.

Another way could be that you see a Found Windows Media Center Extender balloon appear above your task bar.

1 Click the balloon for more information

Hot tip

It doesn't matter which option you use to start the process to add an extender, as they all launch the same add extender wizard.

2 Click Yes to launch the add extender wizard

Network Performance

The Network Performance Tuner allows you to verify that you have enough available network bandwidth to successfully use an extender to connect to Windows Media Center and have a usable experience. This is because high quality TV and video sent between the Windows Media Center and the Extender requires significantly more bandwidth than what you would normally use for surfing the Internet or sending emails.

1 On the Tune Your Network screen, select Yes (recommended) to run the Network Performance Tuner

2 On the Welcome to the Network Performance Tuner screen, click Next to start measuring network performance

The network will now be tested – this may take a few minutes so be patient. You will then either receive an acceptable network performance rating or a poor network performance rating.

3 Select Yes to view your network bandwidth and click Next

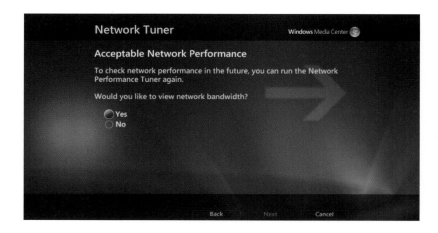

4 On the Network Performance Monitor screen, select either Bar view or Graph view and click Next to view the network performance to see a real-time view of the network

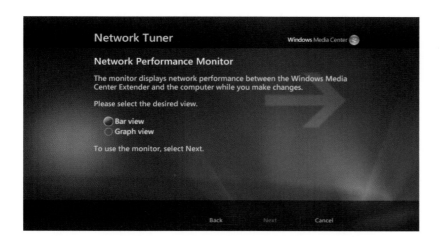

5 Make any changes to your network, especially if you are using Wireless, until the network performance is acceptable for what you intend to use it for, then click Next

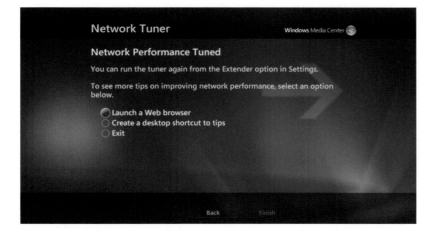

Hot tip

You can run the Network Performance Tuner at any time by selecting Tasks, Options, Extender, selecting the Extender device and clicking on Tune network.

6 If you want to see any tips on improving network performance select Launch a Web browser or Create a desktop shortcut to tips

7 Click Exit to finish and exit the Network Performance Tuner

Network Bandwidth Views

You can then view the network performance between your Extender and your Windows Media Center computer. This is useful if you are going to make any changes as you can see the effects in real-time. You can choose between Bar view or Graph view.

Bar view

Bar view is very useful in seeing a quick snapshot of your network.

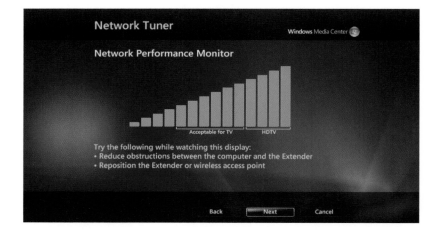

Graph view

Graph view is useful to see a rolling view of your network performance so that when you make any changes you can see exactly what the effect is.

Settings

Once you have setup and configured the connection to the Windows Media Center Extender, there are a couple of different options available to you.

1 From the main menu, select Tasks, settings, Extender

Hot tip

If your Extender is not switched on or if there are network connectivity issues, you will be able to see it from here.

2 Select the Extender you wish to use

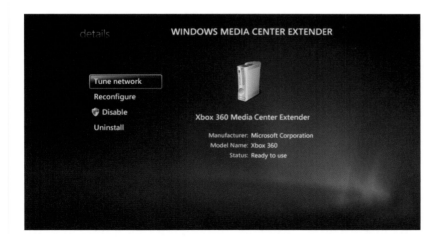

Hot tip

You can rerun the Network Performance Tuner by selecting Tune network.

From here you can see the manufacturer, model name and status of the selected Windows Media Center Extender.

...cont'd

Disabling an Extender

You can disable an Extender, rather than uninstalling it if you wish. That way in order to use it again in the future, you just have to enable it again.

1 Select Disable in order to disable the Extender

2 To enable it again in the future, just select Enable

Don't forget

If you disable or uninstall an Extender, anyone who is using that Extender to connect to your Windows Media Center computer will be disconnected.

Uninstalling an Extender

If you are sure you no longer want the Extender connected to your Windows Media Center computer, you can uninstall it.

1 Select Uninstall in order to remove the Extender

2 Click Next on the Extender Uninstall screen

The Extender is now uninstalled and any settings associated with the device are removed.

Adding a new Extender

From here you can easily add a new Extender by selecting the add extender button or you can navigate back to the main menu and select add extender from the Tasks menu.

Remote Controls

You can control your Media Center Extender using a variety of remote controls, including the Windows Media Center remote control, an Xbox 360 remote control or even the Xbox 360 controller itself.

Setting up the Windows Media Center Remote
If you want to use the Windows Media Center remote control on your Xbox 360, the following steps need to be performed on the Xbox 360:

1 Go to the System blade

2 Select Console Settings

3 Select Remote Control

4 Select All Channels

To stop using the Windows Media Center remote control, just select Xbox 360 Media Remote from the menu.

Using Remotes to Enter Text
If you need to enter text onto the Xbox 360, you can either use the Xbox 360 onscreen keyboard or you can use the numeric keypad on any of the remote controls.

To display the onscreen keyboard, press the DVD MENU button on the remote control or the Y button on the Xbox 360 controller.

More Info
When you press the More Info button on a remote control, you get additional menu options specific to wherever you are and whatever you are doing at the time. In order to get the same More Info experience when using the Xbox 360 controller, just press the X button.

Don't forget

If you decide you only want to use the Xbox 360 Media remote control in the future, follow the same steps only select Xbox 360 Media Remote instead.

Beware

The Windows Media Center remote control cannot be used to adjust the volume on the Xbox 360, you will need to use the Xbox 360 controller to do this.

Beware

If you have your Windows Media Center computer and your Windows Media Center Extender in the same room, when you use one of the remote controls you may experience both devices being controlled at the same time from your remote control.

Troubleshooting

If you are having problems connecting your Windows Media Center Extender to your Windows Media Center computer, there are a number of different troubleshooting steps you could try.

Network Issues

Ensure that your Xbox 360 console is connected to your home network, either via an Ethernet cable or via a wireless connection. You can check to see if your Xbox 360 has a valid IP address:

1 From the System blade, select Network Settings

2 Select Edit Settings to view the IP and DNS settings

You are looking for an IP address and Subnet mask that matches your network configuration, along with the correct DNS entries. You can test settings by checking the connection to Xbox Live:

3 Select Test Xbox Live Connection from the Network Settings menu and confirm you want to continue to run the tests

You are looking to see the word Confirmed against each of the tests. If any say Failed, click on the More Info button for additional information and troubleshooting steps.

Xbox 360 Issues

A fairly common problem appears if you have connected your Xbox 360 to a Media Center 2005 computer and used it as an Extender. It will stop you from connecting to Windows Media Center. To resolve this issue:

1 From the System blade, select Memory and select the storage device you are using

2 Select Games and then Xbox 360 Dashboard

3 Select Windows Media Center Game and choose Delete

Hot tip

Consider using DHCP to automatically assign all the required IP address details, if you are not already doing so.

Hot tip

Ensure you have downloaded and installed any Xbox 360 updates, as these often include program enhancements and fixes for problems.

Hot tip

You can also check to see if there is an existing connection to a Windows Media Center computer by going to the System blade and selecting Computers, Windows Media Center. If you are connected to one, select Windows Media Center and click on Disconnect.

11 Settings

This chapter will guide you through the various settings that can be configured within Windows Media Center including DVD and Music options, how Windows Media Center looks and behaves and also how to use the Parental Control feature to protect your children from unwanted content.

The Settings Menu

There are a considerable amount of settings that can be configured in Windows Media Center. These include General settings, such as setup and optimization, TV settings for the Guide, and many more.

1 From the Windows Media Center menu, scroll through the options until you get to Tasks and then scroll along to and select Settings

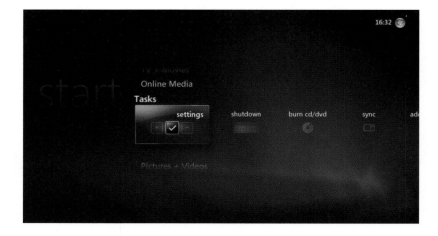

Hot tip

Any of these settings can be changed at any time.

2 From the main Settings menu, highlight the option you want to drill down to and press the OK button on the remote control

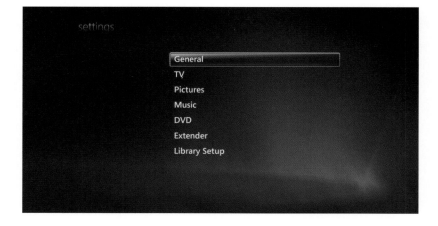

Behavior

The Startup and Window Behavior option allows you to decide how Windows Media Center acts with Windows Vista. Specifically, the settings are:

- Windows Media Center window always on top

- Show "Not designed for Windows Media Center" dialog

- Start Windows Media Center when Windows starts (which will automatically launch Windows Media Center for you)

- Show taskbar notifications (such as when the Guide updates are being downloaded or when CDs or DVDs are being written)

1 Select Startup and Window Behavior from the General menu

Hot tip

If you are only planning on using this computer for Windows Media Center, select Start Windows Media Center when Windows starts.

157

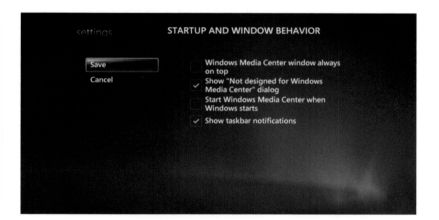

2 Check or Clear the boxes for the options you want

3 Click Save to return to the General menu

You can also manually resize the Windows Media Center window by clicking on the Restore button on the menu bar and then pressing and dragging the resize handle in the lower-right corner of the Window.

Hot tip

You can make the menu bar appear at anytime by moving the mouse. After a few seconds the menu bar will disappear again.

Visual and Sound Effects

The Visual and Sound Effects options are used to set whether or not Windows Media Center uses animations and sounds within the software. You can also change the color scheme and the video background color if you wish.

Specifically, the settings are:

- Use transition animations (these are the animations that appear when you are scrolling through the menu options)
- Play sounds when navigating Windows Media Center
- Color scheme (the choices are Windows Media Center standard, high contrast white or high contract black)
- Video background color (the choices range from white, percentages of gray 10% to 90% through to black)

Hot tip

High contrast is designed for people who are visually impaired. If you, or anyone who will be using Windows Media Center is visually impaired, switch on High contrast.

Beware

High contrast is not available when viewing through either a standard television or a Windows Media Center Extender.

Hot tip

If you are experiencing performance issues with your Windows Media Center computer, try switching off the animations and sounds.

1 Select Visual and Sound Effects from the General menu

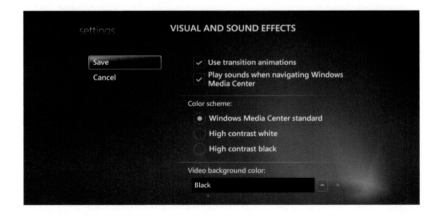

2 Check or clear the boxes for animations and sounds

3 Select the Color scheme you want to use

4 Select the Video background color you want to use

5 Click Save to return to the General menu

Program Library Options

The Program Library, which is part of the Online Media menu contains a number of applications, including games that appear on your Windows Media Center. You can control which applications appear as well as what they can do using these options:

1 Select Program Library Options from the General menu

2 Check or clear the options you want to change

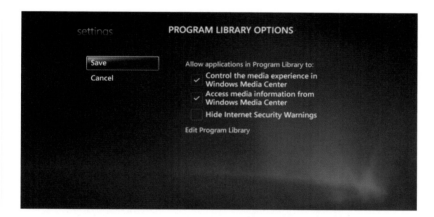

3 If you want to change the applications that appear in the Program Library, click Edit Program Library and check or clear the box as required, then click Save twice

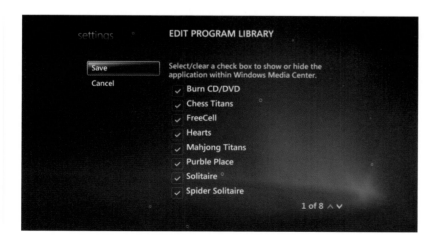

Hot tip

If you have a large number of programs available in the Program Library, you should remove any that you do not use so that it does not become unusable.

WMC Setup

If you want to rerun the setup of any of the setup options within Windows Media Center, you can do so from the Windows Media Center Setup menu. Also, if during the initial and advanced setup you decided to skip a step, you can easily complete that step now.

1 Select Windows Media Center Setup from the menu

2 Select the option you want to run

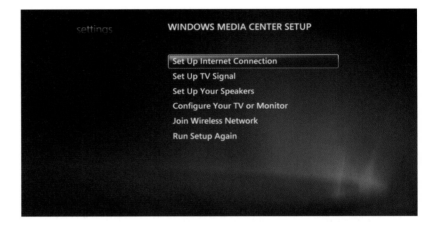

3 If you want to rerun the entire Setup process again, select Run Setup Again

Beware

If you choose to rerun the setup process, all of your existing configuration settings will be lost and you will have to reconfigure all of them again.

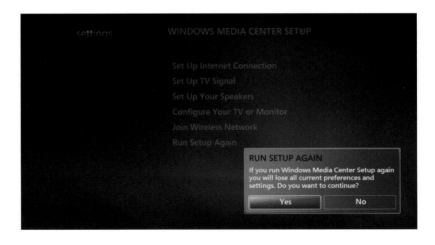

Parental Controls

If you have children, you may want to limit the type of DVD content that they can watch. For example, if your children are not allowed to watch anything over a PG rating (or PG-13 in the US) you can set the maximum allowed movie rating to be PG or PG-13 and any movie that has a rating above that will not be played.

Beware

Parental Controls are not available in all Countries or Regions.

1 Select Parental Controls from the General menu

2 If this is the first time you have been here, enter a 4-digit access code, and then confirm it

settings   CREATE AN ACCESS CODE

@'. abc def
1   2   3
ghi jkl mno
4   5   6
pqrs tuv wxyz
7   8   9

0

CLEAR

Enter a new 4-digit access code
••••
Confirm new access code
•••

You must create an access code to block selected programs from being viewed. Enter the code when you want to view a blocked program.

Beware

Ensure your 4-digit access code is not easily guessed otherwise it could easily be removed without your knowledge or approval.

3 If this is not the first time you have been here, just enter your existing 4-digit access code

The Parental Controls menu gives you the option to enforce DVD Ratings (or remove enforcements), change the Access Code or even reset the parental controls all together.

4 Select DVD Ratings

Hot tip

You can also block all Unrated movies just to be safe!

From here you will be able to select whether or not to turn on movie blocking, and if you do turn it on, set the maximum allowed movie content to be played.

...cont'd

Beware

DVD Ratings are only enforced on DVD movies that support the rating system. If you have recorded the movie yourself it will not be blocked. To get around this, select Block Unrated Movies from the DVD Ratings screen.

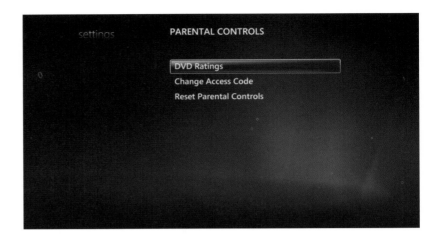

5 If you want to enforce DVD Ratings, check the Turn on movie blocking box

Don't forget

You can change your Access Code at any time by selecting Change Access Code from the Parental Controls Menu.

6 If you want to block unrated movies, check the Block unrated movies box

7 Use the - and + buttons on the screen to select the Maximum allowed movie rating

8 Click Save to return to the Parental Controls menu

Automatic Downloads

There are a couple of options that you can enable to enhance your Windows Media Center experience and the Automatic Download Options is one of them.

These options allow you to select whether or not information about CD album art, media information for DVDs and movies and other useful information is automatically retrieved from the Internet.

You can also select whether certain information, such as that used by the Guide, is downloaded whenever your Windows Media Center computer is connected to the Internet or you can start those downloads manually.

Don't forget

In order to automatically retrieve information from the Internet, your Windows Media Center computer must have an Internet connection.

1 Select Automatic Download Options from the General menu

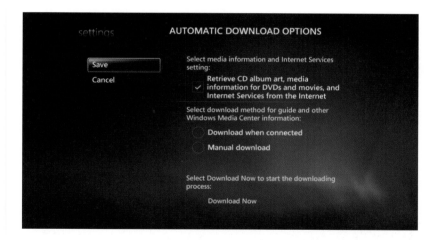

Hot tip

You can initiate a download from this menu by selecting Download Now.

2 Check or clear the Select media information and Internet Services setting depending on whether you want to automatically retrieve content

3 Select the download method for the Guide and other Windows Media Center information

4 Click Save to return to the General menu

Hot tip

To get the best experience and most up to date information, select the Download when connected option and the Retrieve CD album art, media information for DVDs and movies and Internet Services from the Internet option.

Optimization

The Optimization option does exactly what it says – it optimizes your Windows Media Center computer.

The reason for optimization is to ensure that your Windows Media Center computer performs reliably and efficiently.

The optimization takes place at a configurable time each day so you can set it to a time that is convenient for you.

The optimization actually consists of stopping and restarting some of the key Windows Media Center services – effectively performing a soft reboot of the software.

If you always switch off your Windows Media Center computer at the end of each day then you really don't need to worry about setting the optimization as restarting Windows Media Center essentially performs the same function.

Beware

Make sure you set the optimization schedule to a time that you would not normally be using Windows Media Center. You will not be able to use it while optimization takes place.

Don't forget

The optimization schedule is based on the 24 hour clock – so 4:00 is actually 4am.

Hot tip

Make sure you switch the perform optimization function on, as it is surprising how much more reliable Windows Media Center becomes when it is used regularly.

1 Select Optimization from the General menu

WINDOWS MEDIA CENTER OPTIMIZATION

settings

Save
Cancel

To keep your computer running smoothly, optimization tasks are performed regularly on Windows Media Center. During the optimization tasks, you will not be able to use Windows Media Center or Windows Media Center Extender.

☑ Perform Optimization

Optimization Schedule:
4 : 00

2 If you want to perform optimization, check the Perform Optimization box

3 Set the time you want the optimization to commence

4 Click Save to return to the General menu

About Media Center

The About Windows Media Center option is used to see which version of Windows Media Center you are using. You can also view the Guide Terms of Service and the Data Provider Credits.

1 Select About Windows Media Center from the menu

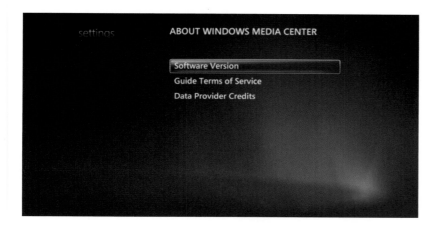

2 Select Software Version to display not only the version details of Windows Vista that you are running, but also some limited information about the computer itself

3 Click Back to return to the menu

Hot tip

Make a note of the information displayed in the Software Version screen as it might be useful later if you need to troubleshoot a problem.

Privacy

The last of the General menu options is Privacy. From here you can view the Online Windows Media Center Privacy Statement, change the Privacy Settings that Windows Media Center uses and also change the Customer Experience Settings.

1 Select Privacy from the menu

2 Select Privacy Settings

3 Check or clear the options depending on how comfortable you are with them, then click Save

Beware

Even though the Guide information sent to Microsoft is anonymous, make sure you are happy about this being sent before you tick the box.

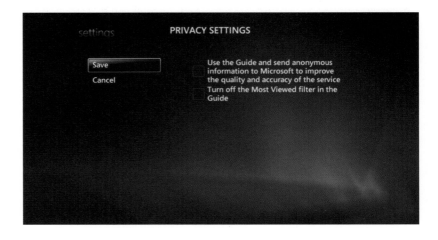

Music Options

The Music options allow you to change what visualizations are used and displayed when listening to music.

1 Select Music from the settings menu

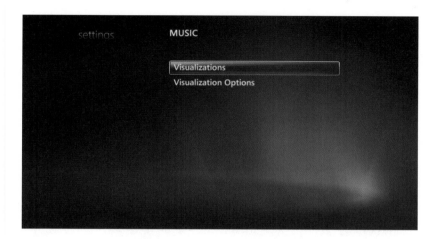

2 Select Visualizations from the Music settings menu

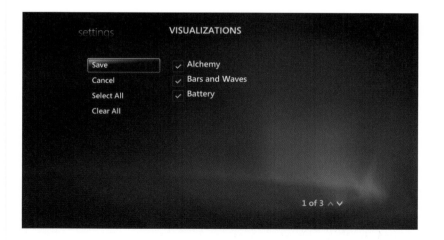

Hot tip

Although it appears as though there are only three visualizations, each one of them has a number of different variations.

3 Check or clear the visualizations you want to have displayed and then click Save

...cont'd

4 Select Visualization Options from the Music settings menu

5 Check the Always start visualizations when music plays box, if you want this option

6 Choose the option for when the song information is shown during the visualization, then click Save

An example of the Battery: Strawberryaid visualization is shown below. Some visualizations are much more interesting than others.

Hot tip

You can change which visualization is being displayed by using the up, down, left and right buttons on your Windows Media Center remote control.

DVD Options

From this group of settings, you can set the language options for
DVD playback, when Closed Captioning (or Subtitles depending
on where you are in the world) is displayed and also change
some of the button functions on your remote control for DVD
playback.

 Select DVD from the settings menu

DVD Language
This option allows you to change the language settings from the
Title Default (the main language track on the DVD) to another
language for subtitles, audio track and the menu.

Don't forget

Depending on what part
of the world you are in,
this menu option might
be called Subtitles.

Don't forget

The DVD you are
watching must support
Closed Captioning
in order for Closed
Captioning to be
displayed.

...cont'd

1 Select DVD Language from the DVD menu

2 Click the - and + buttons on the screen to change the language as appropriate (there are currently 70 different languages to choose from), then click Save

Closed Captioning

This option allows you to choose when closed captioning is displayed, and also which captioning channel to use.

There are three settings for when closed captioning is displayed:

● On when muted (which displays the captioning only when the sound has been muted)

● On (which displays the captioning all the time)

● Off (which does not display the captioning)

There are two settings for which captioning channel is used:

● CC1 or ● CC2

1 Select Closed Captioning from the DVD menu

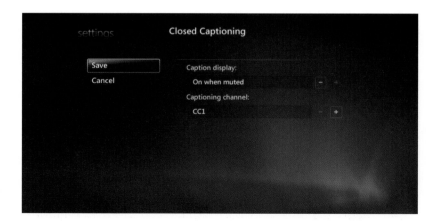

Don't forget

You can only choose a language that is available on the DVD you are playing back, otherwise the Title Default will be used.

170

2 Click the - and + buttons on the screen to change the settings as appropriate, then click Save

Remote Control Options

The last menu option in the DVD Settings menu is Remote Control Options.

The menu option allows you to set how the Program Skip and Replay buttons, and the Program Channel Up and Down buttons behave during the playback of DVD movies.

The available settings are:

- Skip chapters
- Skip forward and back
- Change angles

Depending on which button you press, the resulting action will match. For example, if you set the Program Channel Up and Down buttons to Skip forward and back, when you press the Up button, it will skip forward, and the Down button will skip back.

1 Select Remote Control Options from the DVD settings menu

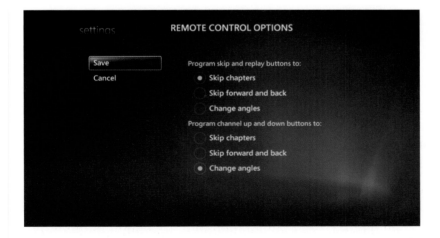

2 Select the option for the Program skip and replay buttons and the Program channel up and down buttons

3 Click Save to return to the DVD menu

Extenders

The Extender settings allow you to configure, uninstall, disable and even add Windows Media Center Extenders to your Windows Media Center computer.

The other option available is whether or not to display notifications when Windows Media Center Extenders are found on your network.

1 Select Extender from the settings menu

2 Select options and check or clear the box depending on your choice. Click Save to return to the menu

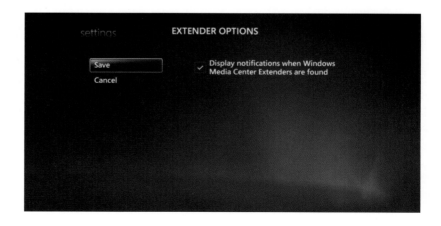

12 TV & Guide Settings

TV

Similar to the General menu, the TV menu consists of a large number of configurable options relating to TV.

These include:

- Recorder
- Guide
- Set Up TV Signal
- Configure Your TV or Monitor
- Audio
- Subtitles

Beware

Some menu options may not appear. This may be because you have not set up some of the functions or that you don't have the correct hardware installed for a particular function, such as a TV tuner card.

1 From the main Settings menu select TV

2 Highlight the option you want to expand and press the OK button on the remote control

Most of these options will be covered in this Chapter, however, the Set Up TV Signal, Scan for More Services and Configure Your TV or Monitor have already been covered in previous Chapters and so won't be covered here.

Recorder

The Recorder options are used to specify the settings for where recorded TV programs are stored and the specific settings used to record them, along with the location of where recorded TV programs can be found.

1 Select Recorder from the TV settings menu

Recorder Storage

You can select the drive you wish to record to, the maximum amount of drive space to use for TV and the recording quality.

1 Select Recorder Storage from the Recorder menu

You can see how much recording time is available from here, in both the amount of time and also the amount of drive space.

...cont'd

Hot tip

If you have the space available, always record in Best quality. If you are running short of available space, consider archiving some of the content to DVD.

Beware

If you only have one drive, or you are recording TV content to your main drive, do not set the maximum TV limit to the same total amount as the drive itself otherwise you might experience problems running your computer.

Don't forget

The folders you set here are only for viewing recorded TV from, they are not for actual recording TV.

2 Select the drive you want to record to

3 Select the maximum amount of drive space to use for TV

4 Select the recording quality

5 Click Save to return to the Recorder menu

More TV Locations

This option allows you to specify additional folders that Windows Media Center will search for when looking for recorded TV content.

1 Select More TV Locations from the Recorder menu

2 Select Add folder to watch and click Next

3 In exactly the same way you added folders to watch as part of the Media Discovery process, work your way through the folder structure on your Windows Media Center computer and place a check against any folder or folders you want to watch, then click Next, then click Finish to start watching the selected folders

Recording Defaults

From here you can specify the default settings for general recordings and also for series only recordings.

General Recording Defaults
The following defaults can be set:

- Keep (the ability to set automatic deletion of content)

- Quality (recording quality from fair to best)

- Start when possible (from on time up to 4 minutes before)

- Stop when possible (from on time up to 4 minutes after)

- Preferred Audio Language

Series Only Recording Defaults
The following defaults can be set:

- Show type (Live, First run or First run and rerun)

- Channels (One channel only or all channels)

- Airtime (Anytime, once per day to a specific time)

- Keep up to (from one recording to as many as possible)

1 Select Recording Defaults from the Recorder menu

2 Work through each of the settings making changes where required, then click Save

Hot tip

So that you don't miss the start or the end of a TV program (if there are any broadcast delays) it is a very good idea to set the Start and Stop, when possible, to the maximum 4 minutes before and after.

Beware

If you like to watch what you record more than once, do not set any automatic deletion on the recorded TV content.

Hot tip

If you only want to record the first time a TV show in a series is broadcast, rather than 'reruns, select First run on the show type setting.

Guide

The Guide options are used to set up the Guide, change the order that the channels are shown, add missing channels, and more.

The specific menu options you should see listed are:

- Change Channel Order
- Edit Channels
- Add Missing Channels
- Restore Channel Defaults
- Set Up Guide Listings
- Get Latest Guide Listings
- Guide Terms of Service
- About Guide Listings

Don't forget

Some of the menu options displayed in the Guide settings may only be available once you have actually configured the Guide.

1 Select Guide from the TV settings menu

2 Select whichever menu item you want to change (they will be covered over the next few pages)

Guide Terms of Service and About Guide Listings provide information specific to the provider of the Guide listings – they do not have any options to change, they are purely informational.

Guide Listing Updates

The Guide listings can be updated at any time by selecting Set Up Guide Listings from the Guide menu.

TV service providers can update the channels they provide at any time, and as such it is advisable on a regular basis to update the Guide listings. Also, depending on whether you selected download when connected or manual download during the initial setup of Windows Media Center, you might need to manually initiate a download.

Hot tip

You will only see the Get Latest Guide Listings option on the Guide menu once you have set up the Guide.

1 Select Get Latest Guide Listings from the Guide menu

2 Select Yes to begin the download process

Don't forget

Windows Media Center will need a connection to the Internet in order to download the Guide listings updates.

3 You will then be advised the Guide listings download is in progress. Click OK to continue

Hot tip

While the Guide listings are being updated, you can continue to use Windows Media Center.

4 When the Guide listings have downloaded successfully, click OK to finish

Channels

There are a few options available relating to channels, including changing the order, editing them, adding missing channels and even restoring the channel defaults.

Change Channel Order
The Change Channel Order menu option allows you to change the order in which the channels appear in Windows Media Center.

1   Select Change Channel Order from the Guide menu

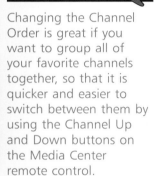

Hot tip

Changing the Channel Order is great if you want to group all of your favorite channels together, so that it is quicker and easier to switch between them by using the Channel Up and Down buttons on the Media Center remote control.

2   Scroll through the list of channels and change the order wherever you want to by clicking on the up and down arrows to the right of each channel name

3   Click Save to return to the Guide menu

Edit Channels
The Edit Channels menu option allows you to add and remove channels as they appear within Windows Media Center both in the Guide and also when you are channel surfing.

1   Select Edit Channels from the Guide menu

...cont'd

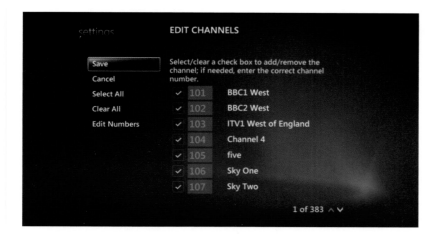

Hot tip

When you remove a channel, the channel listing remains so that if you change your mind at a later stage, you can easily add it back by checking the box again.

2 Scroll through the list and clear the check box for any channels you want to remove

3 If you want to add any channels that you have previously removed, check the box for the required channel

4 Click Save to return to the Guide menu

Depending on your TV Signal source, you may also have the option to edit the numbers of the channels listed.

Hot tip

To save time and make your channel surfing more enjoyable, remove any channels that you are not interested in watching or that are listed as not available depending on your TV Signal source and your subscription (where applicable).

Restoring Channel Defaults

The Restore Channel Defaults option is used to effectively reset the channel list to how it originally was when you first set it up. This is very useful if you have made a large number of changes and you would like to remove those changes in a single action.

1 Select Restore Channel Defaults from the Guide menu

2 Select OK to continue

Beware

Only select the Restore Channel Defaults option if you are really sure, as if you change your mind afterwards you will have to enter every single change you made again.

Adding Missing Channels

If you find that there are missing channels in the Guide, you can add them manually yourself.

1 Select Add Missing Channels from the Guide menu

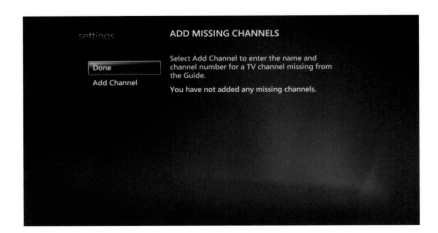

Hot tip

Have a copy of a local TV Guide available to check that you have all of the available channels configured on your Windows Media Center.

2 Select Add Channel

3 Enter the name of the missing channel by using the keyboard or the numeric keypad on the remote control and click Next

4 Depending on your TV signal source, you will be asked to enter either the frequency for the channel name you entered (if you are using an antenna) or the channel number (if you are using cable or satellite)

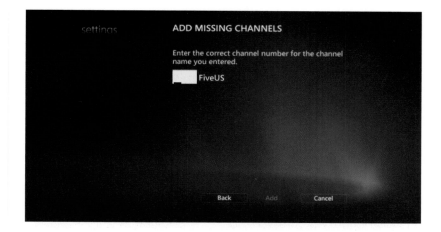

183

Don't forget

You will need to know either the frequency or the channel number for each of the missing channels.

5 Click Add

6 Repeat these steps for each missing channel

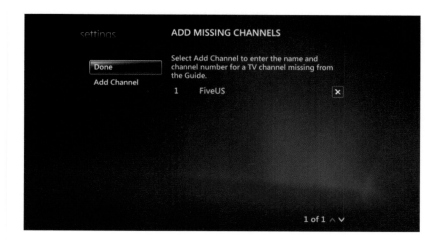

Hot tip

If you make a mistake or change your mind about a certain channel, just click the X button next to each channel to remove it.

7 Click Done to return to the Guide menu

TV Audio

From the TV audio menu, you can select between Stereo and SAP. SAP (which stands for Second Audio Program) allows a TV station to broadcast other information, such as the soundtrack in a different language or even information such as the weather or Descriptive Video Services (DVS) for the visually impaired.

Beware

SAP is only supported on displays that are capable of playing Stereo sound.

1 Select Audio from the TV menu

2 Select between Stereo and SAP

3 Click Save to return to the TV menu

Reconfiguring Displays

The Configure Your TV or Monitor menu item enables you to run or rerun the Display Configuration wizard.

Rerunning the wizard can be very useful if you have changed your display or if you have experienced any playback problems.

Hot tip

For more information on the Display Configuration Wizard see Chapter 4.

1 Select Configure Your TV or Monitor from the TV menu

Subtitles

Subtitles are when the spoken audio on a TV program is displayed in text on the screen. This can be used by the hard of hearing or the deaf in order to know what is being said on the TV program or movie.

①   Select Subtitle from the TV menu

②   Select when to display subtitles – the choices are Only when muted (which is the default setting), Off or On all the time

③   Enter the Teletext subtitle page number (if appropriate to your region – for example if you are in the United Kingdom the Teletext subtitle page for that channel might be page 888)

Depending on which region you are in, you might not see the Teletext subtitle page box. You might see a Basic Captioning box or you might see a Preferred Language box. If this is the case make any settings changes that are appropriate for your region.

④   Click Save to return to the TV menu

Don't forget

Depending on what region you are in, Subtitles might be referred to as Closed Captioning.

Don't forget

Subtitles are only available for programs that have them provided as part of the broadcast. Not all programs will have subtitles.

Beware

If you are using DVB-T then subtitles are not currently supported.

Changing TV Signals

You can also either run the TV Signal Setup for the first time or you can rerun again by selecting the Set Up TV Signal option.

1 Select Set Up TV Signal from the TV menu

If you have previously configured the TV Signal then you will see a warning:

2 Select either Yes to rerun the setup or No to return to the TV menu

3 If you selected Yes, run through the same TV Signal Setup steps as you did before (see Chapter 3 for more information on how to do this if you are unsure)

Multi-tuner Configurations

Depending on your location, Windows Media Center can support up to four TV tuners (as long as your computer can actually hold four TV tuners).

The United States is currently the only location that can support four TV tuners with the rest of the world only being able to support two TV tuners.

For each of the tuners, the levels of support are:

● Dual ATSC +

● Dual NTSC (both signals are the same)

● Dual digital cable tuners (with or without CableCARDs)

Hot tip

If you add an additional TV tuner card, or you change your TV signal source, run the Set Up TV Signal option again.

Beware

Running the Set Up TV Signal option will remove all existing settings related to your TV signal.

Beware

Do not change your TV Signal settings while you are either watching or recording TV as you will lose the signal.

Index